better ways to read the bible

Transforming a Weapon of Harm into a Tool of Healing

zach w. lambert

BrazosPress
a division of Baker Publishing Group
Grand Rapids, Michigan

Published by Brazos Press
a division of Baker Publishing Group
Grand Rapids, Michigan
BrazosPress.com

Printed in the United States of America

Library of Congress Cataloging-in-Publication Data
Names: Lambert, Zach W., 1988- author.
Title: Better ways to read the Bible : transforming a weapon of harm into a tool of healing / Zach W. Lambert.
Description: Grand Rapids, Michigan : Brazos Press, a division of Baker Publishing Group, 2025. | Includes bibliographical references.
Identifiers: LCCN 2025003379 | ISBN 9781587436680 (paperback) | ISBN 9781493450305 (ebook)
Subjects: LCSH: Bible—Reading.
Classification: LCC BS617 .L23 2025 | DDC 220—dc23/eng/20250215
LC record available at https://lccn.loc.gov/2025003379

Some identifying details of subjects whose stories are included in this book have been changed to protect their privacy. Stories are retold to the best of the author's recollection.

Cover design by Faceout Studio, Molly von Borstel
Interior design by William Overbeeke

Author is represented by The Christopher Ferebee Agency, www.christopherferebee.com.

Baker Publishing Group publications use paper produced from sustainable forestry practices and postconsumer waste whenever possible.

26 27 28 29 30 31   8 7 6 5 4

"Lambert challenges the ways Scripture has been misused and invites readers into a more compassionate, justice-centered understanding of the Bible."

—**Brit Barron**, author of *Do You Still Talk to Grandma?*

"This fine debut book by leading post-evangelical pastor Zach Lambert is a profound combination of memoir, biblical storytelling, and scriptural interpretation. It will be a major resource for the rapidly growing community of post-evangelicals. I highly recommend this work!"

—**David P. Gushee**, professor, Mercer University

"In *Better Ways to Read the Bible*, Zach Lambert does what so many Christian leaders seem unwilling to do: he asks tough, important questions of the Bible and opens himself to unexpected responses. With a theologian's mind and a pastor's heart, Lambert shares his personal, often painful, stories from his journey of relearning Scripture. This book offers a fresh reading of the Bible that provides a counternarrative to white Christian nationalism and its rigid, exclusionary interpretations of the teachings of God. What emerges is a vision of the kind of Christianity most people imagine and hope for in the world. This book is for the faithful, the skeptic, and the inquirer. No matter who you are, this book will make you curious about another book: the Bible."

—**Jemar Tisby**, historian, professor, and *New York Times* bestselling author of *The Color of Compromise*

"This book is for those who have been harmed by the church; it will bring healing. This book is for those who will not agree with it; it will bring understanding. This book is for those who can't reconcile the words of Christ to love God and love others with the church they see today; it will bring clarity. With pastoral compassion and wit, Zach Lambert invites you into a conversation about how the Bible can be read differently. He will challenge you, encourage you, and show you how, even amid theological differences, Christians should be known first for our love."

—**Beth Allison Barr**, professor, Baylor University; bestselling author of *The Making of Biblical Womanhood* and *Becoming the Pastor's Wife*

"This book is a must-read for anyone wrestling with faith after experiencing harmful Bible interpretations. Lambert offers a path forward, transforming Scripture from a weapon of harm into a healing tool. With clarity and compassion, he exposes problematic lenses and provides practical alternatives. Lambert's unveiling offers hope for the marginalized and tools for healthy Bible reading. This book will empower readers to reclaim the Bible as a source of liberation and wholeness."

—**Latasha Morrison**, *New York Times* bestselling author of *Be the Bridge*

"It's been said that many Christians have a head full of Scripture but a heart full of hate. That is why I find Zach Lambert so refreshing. In this debut book, he answers bad theology with good theology. Zach is a pastor who loves people and a theologian who loves Scripture. He cares so much about Jesus and the Bible that he isn't willing to concede his faith to those who distort Scripture in order to camouflage their bigotry. This is a book for people who love the Bible as much as it is a book for those who have been turned off by the Bible because of how it's been weaponized. Let it cause you to lean in, stay curious, question the clichés, and take the Bible back as a love story."

—**Shane Claiborne**, author, activist, and cofounder of Red Letter Christians

"Many are disturbed at the rapid rate at which the Bible, especially in the United States, is being used as a weapon. Rooted in his own personal experience, deep study, and pastoral ministry, Zach Lambert offers sage guidance for moving beyond the harmful lenses that obscure and distort the life-affirming words of Scripture. This book is a winsome and insightful aid for followers of Jesus."

—**Peter Enns**, professor, Eastern University; host of *The Bible for Normal People* podcast; author of *The Bible Tells Me So* and *How the Bible Actually Works*

For Amy

You are my best friend
and the best writer in our family.
I couldn't have done this,
or anything else in my life,
without you.

contents

foreword

by Sarah Bessey

If you were introduced to the Bible as an answer book or as a manual for a prosperous life, well, how's that going for you?

For those of us who came of age with a version of Christianity that depends on certainty, like-mindedness, and answer-book faith, when we lose that certainty, it can feel like we've lost God altogether. In all my years alongside people doing the good, difficult work of reimagining their faith, I can attest that nowhere is that disorientation more felt than in our relationship with the Scriptures.

Building a faith that depends on narrow boxes for God may work for a time, but eventually real life happens to us all. Your church has become a political action committee that you no longer recognize, the prayer isn't answered, the memorized Romans Road feels inadequate in the face of suffering, and the story of Abraham nearly sacrificing Isaac horrifies you as you turn the pages of the children's Bible you bought for your toddler.

Perhaps it is then that you find us.

You find the misfits and doubters, the question-askers and so-called troublemakers. You find the ones who asked "But what about . . . ?" in church too often. You find bleeding hearts and social justice warriors, burned-out pastors' wives with a lot of thoughts on patriarchy, purity culture dropouts, liberation theologians and womanists, and gay folks who love and follow Jesus better than your churchy friends, and, well, here you are.

You also find people like Zach Lambert, who was once kicked out of church as a teenager for being a heretic (impressive; it took me until my late twenties to be regularly called a heretic, so clearly you are in the presence of a prodigy) and is now a pastor and theologian.

Welcome. Welcome. We're so glad you're here. You're right on time. Yes, when you find yourself among those whose faith has lost its shine, whose certainty becomes a mystery, and whose relationship with the Bible is best described as "it's complicated," you're exactly where you need to be. You're at an altar of encounter with God.

This was certainly my experience. I grew up within the prosperity gospel and Word of Faith movements of the 1980s and '90s. If you needed some naming and/or claiming, some declaring of "the Word" or positive confession or memorized Bible verses to be fired off at will and out of context, then I was your gal. I truly loved my Bible with an intensity reserved for us religious teenagers who equate certainty with faithfulness and belovedness.

When I also entered the healthy and developmentally normal stage of faith of questioning the Bible more than twenty years ago, it was profoundly disorienting. Wasn't my love for Jesus and my love for the Bible supposed to inoculate against doubt? Was this a sign that I wasn't as faithful as I had felt? Perhaps I had been deceived. Or was I in danger of being prideful and of elevating my own understanding over God's Word (or perhaps worse, over my pastor's opinion)?

But no, I had landed in that place of what I now know as deconstruction precisely because God's love was so immediate, so real, so tangible to me, that I couldn't help beginning to grapple with how I was going to embody that hope and goodness, even in my reading of the Bible. As pastor and theologian Jasper Peters said at an Evolving Faith conference a few years ago, "The more God's love took ahold of me, the more difficult it became to read the text [the Bible] in the way that I always had."

I have a hunch that that same difficulty with the Bible is what may have brought you to this book. As God's love took hold of you, the answers that once seemed so secure began to feel trite, the interpretations that once seemed so certain became a source of doubt, and the boundaries that once seemed so settled were expanded. The more we understand and live within the inclusive, welcoming, hospitable, and life-changing love of God, the more we wrestle with an incomplete or even harmful reading of the Bible.

We're not the anomaly, nor are we a cautionary tale. We are part of a faithful story of believers and doubters, church kids and skeptics who begin to understand that to love the Bible, to truly love this ancient library of books, means to honestly wrestle with the Bible. There is so much good life on the other side of that disorientation.

Sadly, most of us have not had the fortunate experience of doing that good, hard work alongside a good pastor who loves God, loves their Bible, and loves us like Zach Lambert does.

There is no shortage of people who will help you tear down what was once precious to you and then dance upon the grave. But it is a rare thing to find a trustworthy guide and shepherd in the next necessary step of reimagining and rebuilding, in the healing and the hope that is possible. Zach is interested in the unlearning that we need to do about the Bible, absolutely, but he isn't content to stop there. He invites us to release the narratives and frameworks for understanding the Bible that cause harm and division. Then he flings open the door wide for a broader, wiser, more grounded understanding of the Bible, one that brings healing, and even perhaps some hope, for all God's children. Learning a better way to read the Bible is part of our work to better love not only God but each other.

None of this is theoretical. How we read the Bible changes how we think, spend our money, vote, show up in our communities, love our neighbors, and so many other aspects of our lives. A bad, incomplete, wicked, or even just selfish reading of the Bible is profoundly dangerous. As Zach writes, "Jesus chastised folks who weaponized Scripture and elevated it above love of neighbor. He repeatedly denounced those who used sacred texts to divide rather than unite, incite violence rather than make peace, and exclude rather than include." Learning how to read the Bible again is not merely a theory to us anymore: this work matters deeply not only in your own heart and life but in the lives of your neighbors and this world God so loves.

God's love is what compelled Zach Lambert to ask those pesky questions in youth group. It's what compelled him to study the Bible years later when he attended seminary. It's what compelled him to give up a position at a megachurch because of the way the Scriptures were being used to harm the most vulnerable and marginalized. It drove him to teachers and companions who reshaped how he read the same Scriptures he once assumed he knew so well. That same love led him to plant a church in Austin to embody that hope and teach folks how to read the Bible in a more whole, healing, inclusive, and, I believe, *biblical* way. And that love is what compelled him to write this book for us. Rejecting the lenses of literalism or moralism or even hierarchy among others, Zach invites us to read the Bible through a lens formed by our revolutionary Jesus, by the context of the particulars, by flourishing, and even by fruitfulness.

What Zach models here is the key to carrying forward this conversation about how we read, interpret, understand, and even apply the Bible: it is humility. Zach is a vigorous thinker, unafraid to shy away from the big questions. But he is also deeply pastoral. Underneath all of these words, you'll find a kind, hospitable, and quiet invitation to curiosity, to wonder, and even to rest in the love of God as we seek to follow Jesus. As Zach says and demonstrates so beautifully in the following pages, the way of Jesus always leads to healing, not harm. And that healing includes how you read and are formed by your Bible.

introduction

How the Bible Beat Me Up

> When religion won't tolerate questions, objections, or differences of opinion and all it can do is threaten excommunication, violence, and hellfire, it has an unfortunate habit of producing some of the most hateful people to ever walk the earth.
>
> —David Dark, *The Sacredness of Questioning Everything*

"Your son is disruptive, disrespectful, and dishonoring to God. He asks too many questions during Bible study, and it's causing the other students to doubt their faith. I'm sorry, but he's not welcome here anymore."

My youth pastor said this to my parents one Wednesday night when they came to pick me up from our Southern Baptist church's youth group. A few minutes prior, I'd been told to go sit in the hallway after asking a "heretical" question during the Bible study portion of the program.

What was the question? It was the week of Easter, and our youth pastor was talking about Jesus's death on the cross. He told us that because Jesus had all our sin laid on him, God the Father had to leave Jesus alone because he[1] can't be around sin.

My hand shot up. Before being called on, I blurted out something to the effect of "Didn't you just say that God was a good father? A good father doesn't turn his back on his son when he needs him most. If God can't be around Jesus because of sin, then he definitely won't want to be around me."

"Go sit in the hallway, Zach," my youth pastor responded, accompanied by an irritated stare I'd become familiar with.

Banishing me from Bible studies or telling me to pray harder was usually the response to my questions about the Bible and my doubts about faith.

But no amount of prayer assuaged my doubts, and no amount of hallway sitting eradicated my questions. My doubts grew bigger and my questions loomed larger. I viscerally understood Christian spaces were not safe places to ask pesky questions or voice nagging doubts, so I spent most of my teenage years searching for answers and meaning elsewhere.

That's when I overdosed.

The summer before my senior year of high school, I overdosed on a combination of alcohol and cough medicine. The very next night, I watched someone else overdose and drown.

These two nights amplified my questions even more; it now felt like acquiring the answers was a matter of life and death. Even though I'd been expelled from every Christian space I'd

1. God transcends both sex and gender. I have chosen to use masculine language when talking about God the Father throughout this book because masculine pronouns are used by the biblical authors. If using "they/them," "she/her," or anything else is helpful for you, by all means please do so as you read along. Attempting to describe our indescribable Creator is not an easy task, and I believe we should be much more gracious with each other as we attempt to do so.

known, I did what any good Christian is supposed to do: I returned to the Bible.

I took a different approach this time, trying to read it with fresh eyes. I started with Matthew, the first book in the New Testament and one of the four Gospels, which tell the story of Jesus's life. I didn't go verse by verse with a commentary or attempt to translate every word from the original language like some pastors have done. I just read it. Like a book. Like a story. And, well, that changed everything.

I began to realize that I knew the beginning and the end of Jesus's story by heart—the stories of his birth at Christmas and his death and resurrection at Easter had been drilled into me—but I knew very little about the rest of Jesus's life. Sure, I'd heard about Jesus walking on water and feeding a bunch of people with just some bread and fish, but outside of that, I was clueless.

I didn't know Jesus was constantly offering alternative interpretations of Scripture, even when other rabbis disagreed with him. I didn't know he was reprimanded for hanging out with people on the margins. I didn't know he taught that love was the most important thing. I didn't know he pushed back against the occupying Roman authorities. I felt like I knew baby Jesus and resurrected Jesus, but I was meeting the radical, revolutionary Jesus for the very first time. This was the Jesus I wanted to follow.

I decided I was going to be a Christian, but what kind would I be? I'd always been told there were three kinds of Christians: Southern Baptists, Roman Catholics, and "crazy liberals," who probably weren't actually Christians. At age seventeen, I knew I wasn't a Catholic or a liberal, so I figured the only other option was to boomerang back into the Southern Baptist world, the only kind of church I'd ever known.

A year later, I finished high school and left Austin to play college football in West Texas, but after a career-ending shoulder injury my freshman year,[2] I became a youth pastor at a small, rural Southern Baptist church, where I worked until I graduated from college. Talk about coming full circle. My wife and I, married all of six months, decided that graduate school was the best next step.

We moved to Dallas, and I started seminary classes on the same day I started a job at one of the largest churches in America. As an intern, I directly supported the senior pastor on everything from sermon composition to dry-cleaning retrieval. During my time on his staff, I saw the Bible weaponized in new and horrific ways.

I'm going to talk a lot about the "weaponization" of Scripture throughout this book, so allow me to offer a brief definition of the term. "Weaponization" is the process of turning something meant to be a tool of healing into an instrument of harm.

The weaponization of Scripture is not theoretical. It happens every single day, with devastating consequences. I will tell stories throughout this book of the Bible being weaponized against people, while exploring better ways to read it, but it's worth sharing an example here as well. Two of my closest friends in Austin are Imam Attia Omara and Rabbi Kelly Levy. The three of us have been working together on multifaith projects for the good of our city since 2020.[3] Both Imam Attia's mosque and Rabbi Kelly's synagogue have been the target of attacks by Christians in the last few years.[4] After one attack on his mosque, Attia

2. My bicep tendon ruptured and rolled back into my elbow. I rushed through recovery so I could play intramural basketball, and sometimes it still hurts today. My girlfriend at the time, who is now my wife, warned me this is what would happen. But I didn't listen. You were right, Amy.

3. We do this through an organization called Multi-Faith Neighbors Network. For more on this, see www.mfnn.org.

4. Office of Public Affairs, US Department of Justice, "Texas Man Pleads Guilty to Hate Crime and Arson for Setting Fire to Synagogue," press release, April 7, 2023, https://www.justice.gov/opa/pr/texas-man-pleads-guilty-hate-crime-and-arson-setting-fire-synagogue; Mary Tuma, "North Austin Mosque Targeted Again,"

texted me a picture of the sign left behind by the assailants. The sign had an artificial pig's head covered in fake blood staked through the top of it and the words "MUSLIMS: You are as unclean to God as a pig is to you. Have your idolatry washed clean by the blood of Jesus Christ! 1 Corinthians 6:9–11."

In case you're wondering, 1 Corinthians 6:9–11 says, "Or do you not know that wrongdoers will not inherit the kingdom of God? Do not be deceived: Neither the sexually immoral nor idolaters nor adulterers nor men who have sex with men nor thieves nor the greedy nor drunkards nor slanderers nor swindlers will inherit the kingdom of God. And that is what some of you were. But you were washed, you were sanctified, you were justified in the name of the Lord Jesus Christ and by the Spirit of our God."

This passage is from a letter written by the apostle Paul to the church in Corinth. The larger section is about not suing fellow Christians, and the verses immediately preceding the passage say this: "The very fact that you have lawsuits among you means you have been completely defeated already. Why not rather be wronged? Why not rather be cheated? Instead, you yourselves cheat and do wrong, and you do this to your brothers and sisters. Or do you not know that wrongdoers will not inherit the kingdom?" (1 Cor. 6:7–9).

The weaponization of Scripture looks like twisting a passage meant to encourage Christians to avoid lawsuits if possible into a justification for violence against Muslims.

Austin Chronicle, May 3, 2019, https://www.austinchronicle.com/news/2019-05-03/north-austin-mosque-targeted-again; Sanya Mansoor, "Two Texas Mosques Burned to the Ground This Month," *Texas Tribune*, January 30, 2017, https://www.texastribune.org/2017/01/30/two-texas-mosques-burned-ground-january; Eric Pointer, "Man Convicted in Connection with 2021 Austin Synagogue Arson Sentenced to 10 Years in Prison," KVUE, November 29, 2023, https://www.kvue.com/article/news/crime/austin-synagogue-suspect-sentencing/269-28733bfe-b3d3-477a-aaba-1d224765e08a.

At the megachurch where I worked, I often saw the Bible weaponized to justify bad behavior by staff members, cover up abuse, promote conversion therapy for LGBTQ+ folks, and much more. These incidents left me shaken and jaded, unsure if I could continue a career in ministry. After two years of watching pastors use the Bible to inflict harm on the very people they were supposed to be caring for, I knew I couldn't be a part of it anymore. Without a clue as to what I would do next, I walked into my boss's office and told him I was done.

I was at a crossroads. I still wanted to follow the radical, revolutionary Jesus, but he was nowhere to be found in so much of the Christianity around me. I also knew I needed to figure out better ways to read the Bible. The ways I'd watched it wielded as a weapon were incongruent with who I knew Jesus to be. But I wasn't ready to throw away the Bible. After all, it's where I first read about the life-changing love of Jesus.

I didn't have the language at the time, but looking back, I see that I was trying to deconstruct harmful ways of reading the Bible and reconstruct something better. This deconstruction and reconstruction process eventually led me to move back to my hometown of Austin to start Restore Austin—a church for the many people who'd been left out in the cold by churches and leaders who mishandled the Scriptures. It didn't take long for me to see that more people fell into this category than I previously realized.

Many folks have come to see the Bible as either a dusty old book that's irrelevant to modern life or a toxic text that causes more harm than good in politics, people's lives, and the public square. Research reveals that the majority of Americans now say they read the Bible "never" or "less than once a year."[5] A

5. Jeffery Fulks, Randy Petersen, and John Farquhar Plake, *State of the Bible: USA 2022* (American Bible Society, 2022), https://1s712.americanbible.org/state-of-the-bible/stateofthebible/State_of_the_bible-2022.pdf.

major reason people are avoiding the Bible is because they have experienced it not as a good book but rather as a weapon to shame and scold, judge and condemn, marginalize and oppress.

A lack of confidence in the goodness of Scripture has led to a lack of confidence in the churches and pastors who preach it. When religious leaders misuse the Bible in ways that inflict pain on people, those people understandably leave. This is one significant reason why the church in America is experiencing the greatest mass exodus in its history.[6]

I knew I wasn't going to change a national trend from my solitary perch in Austin, but I could provide an alternative community where those who had been spiritually burned could find solace and healing. So we founded Restore as a place where anyone has a seat at the table and everyone experiences the love of Jesus. In order to avoid perpetuating harm and triggering trauma for those who had been beaten up by the Bible, myself included, I knew we needed to read and interpret the Bible differently than the communities many of us had come from read it.

Putting on New Lenses

Everyone who reads and interprets the Bible does so with a set of assumptions about what the Bible is and how it's supposed to work. This set of assumptions functions like a filter or a lens through which the reader attempts to make meaning. Although everyone reads the Bible through a lens (or set of lenses)—there is no neutral or unfiltered way to read it—many people are unaware that they're doing so and have never stopped to take stock of the assumptions they bring to the text and how those assumptions impact interpretations.

6. Jeffrey M. Jones, "U.S. Church Membership Falls Below Majority for First Time," Gallup, March 29, 2021, https://news.gallup.com/poll/341963/church-membership-falls-below-majority-first-time.aspx.

As a new pastor, I began to look at the ways I had been taught to read the Bible, including all the assumptions I'd inherited during my childhood and young adulthood. That's when I began to see that I had learned to read the Bible through four distinct lenses that often lead to harm:

1. The literalism lens: "The Bible says it, I believe it, that settles it."
2. The apocalypse lens: "It's all gonna burn anyway."
3. The moralism lens: "Well, that's not biblical."
4. The hierarchy lens: "Submit to authority as you submit to God."

Next, I began to study how other Bible readers in both ancient and modern times—from Jesuits in Latin America to the Black Church in the United States to Christian mystics of the Greco-Roman world—interpreted Scripture. I noticed that their ways of reading the Bible had historically led to greater spiritual wisdom, personal freedom, and communal flourishing. Their common assumptions formed the basis of what I began to call "healthy lenses":

1. The Jesus lens: "The Scriptures point to me."
2. The context lens: "The one who seeks will find."
3. The flourishing lens: "I have come that they may have life abundantly."
4. The fruitfulness lens: "By their fruit you will recognize them."

For more than a decade, the Restore community has learned how to move away from the harmful lenses and lean into these four healthy lenses. We've tested and tried them in Sunday morning sermons, small group discussions, Bible classes, and conversations between friends. And the results have been stunning: People have been set free from toxic interpretations, wounds have been healed, and our community has begun to live out a version of Christianity that actually looks like Jesus.

In the following pages, I'll lead you through this same journey so that you too can discover what a restored reading of the Bible might look like. We'll take these lenses and apply them to frequently weaponized biblical passages, concepts, and statements, like "I do not permit a woman to teach," the creation story in Genesis, the notorious "clobber verses" used against LGBTQ+ people, the book of Revelation, eternal conscious torment in hell, and much more.

To help you along the way, I've included resources for further exploration and questions for self-reflection at www.zachwlambert.org/discussion. I'll also introduce you to people of various ages, races, genders, sexual orientations, abilities, and social standings who have mentored me in this approach to Bible reading. I would not be who I am or where I am without the incredible grace shown to me by many people who appear in this book; they have taught me so much about interpreting Scripture in ways that lead to the fullness of life Jesus desires for all people. I have chosen to use pseudonyms for most of these folks in order to protect their privacy. All their stories are retold to the best of my ability, and the quotations used are to the best of my recollection.

I started this journey because I came to believe that if our way of interpreting the Bible hurts people, then it must be reconsidered. The way of Jesus always leads to healing, not harm. Better ways to read the Bible exist, ways that lead to restoration, wholeness, and flourishing for all people. If you feel similarly and are ready to take a fresh look at the Scriptures, welcome to the journey. Let's discover better ways of reading the Bible together.

part 1

we all have lenses

1

you're reading it wrong

> I have come to regard with some suspicion those who claim that the Bible never troubles them. I can only assume this means they haven't actually read it.
>
> —Rachel Held Evans, *A Year of Biblical Womanhood*

I love the Bible, but honestly, there have been times when I kind of hated it, times when I was mad at it, and even times when I didn't want to open it because I feared what I might find inside. There have been seasons of my life when I curled up with my Bible and felt like I could hear God speaking directly to me through the words of Scripture. There have also been moments when I got so mad at something I read that I threw my Bible across the room.

I'm not the only one who has a complicated relationship with the Bible. I know because I've had countless conversations over the years in which people have expressed just how difficult it can be to engage with Scripture in ways that lead to deeper connection with God and our neighbors.

I've also talked with numerous folks about the spiritual trauma they've endured, and in almost every case, the primary weapon used against them was the Bible. These experiences have led to some people being emotionally and spiritually triggered every time they try to read it, others trudging through Bible study only to be left frustrated or confused, and still others abandoning Scripture altogether. Such realities are nothing new, but our struggles with Scripture have escalated of late.

Every year, the American Bible Society conducts a survey to study how Americans are engaging with Scripture, producing an annual report based on its findings, called *State of the Bible*. The latest report found that roughly twenty-six million people had mostly or completely stopped reading the Bible between 2021 and 2022.[1] This is the sharpest decline on record.

Some of those twenty-six million people are my friends, my fellow church members, and even my pastoral colleagues. One of these friends is Yasmeen. Over coffee, she told me about growing up in the American South with dark skin and a Middle Eastern name. "After 9/11, people said such awful things to me, but the worst things came from Christians."

One young man at her high school told her, "The book of Revelation says Jesus is going to come back and kill everyone who looks like you. After what y'all did to us, I hope it happens soon."

Yasmeen tried to tell him that she was a Christian and that her family had been Christians for generations, but she was shouted down by his friends. Determined to be more equipped for debate the next time something like this happened, Yas-

1. Jeffery Fulks, Randy Petersen, and John Farquhar Plake, *State of the Bible: USA 2022* (American Bible Society, 2022), https://1s712.americanbible.org/state-of-the-bible/stateofthebible/State_of_the_bible-2022.pdf.

meen went to a Christian bookstore to learn more about Revelation. "I walked through the end times theology section and found book after book that basically said exactly what that guy told me. At that point, I was done." Yasmeen decided she would never read the Bible again, because "any book that says God kills people because of where they're from is garbage." Can you blame her?

Roberto and Maria are two more of the twenty-six million. They sat in my office with tears in their eyes and told me about the day their son came out to them. "After he told us he was gay, we didn't know what to do." They went to their Christian counselor for advice.

"I'll never forget it," Maria said. "The counselor opened up her Bible to Leviticus 18, pulled out a marker, and started highlighting verse 22. I hate that verse so much."

Leviticus 18:22 says, "You shall not lie with a male as with a woman. It is an abomination" (NKJV). Roberto and Maria were told that their son stands condemned as an abomination before God. "Unless he stops being gay," the counselor advised, "he will spend eternity in hell." She told them they needed to choose between God and their gay son.

Roberto and Maria chose their son. "That was the last time either of us opened a Bible," they told me. Can you blame them?

The God who put on flesh as Jesus Christ said he came so that absolutely everyone "may have life, and have it to the full" (John 10:10), a life defined by love, joy, peace, goodness, and all the other fruit of God's Spirit at work. As we all know, many people are experiencing the exact opposite at the hands of Christians.

But what if there was another way to read Scripture, one that leads to healing and wholeness in people's lives and spirits? What if there were lenses through which we can interpret the Bible that promote love and liberation rather than exclusion and hate?

What Is the Bible and How Does It Work?

I believe there are. But before we can learn to read the Bible well, we need to understand what it is and how it works. The Bible is often called "God's Word," but this does not mean it is literally filled with God's words. God inspired at least forty human authors across three continents over two thousand years to write down stories attempting to explain who God is, who humans are, God's plan to restore people and all of creation, and how we are to treat each other in the here and now. At various times in the first centuries after the birth of the church, groups of men came together to decide which writings to canonize into the Bible and which to leave out. These processes were messy, to say the least, with violent altercations often breaking out amid heated discussion.

Contrary to popular belief, the Bible is not a book. Yes, it can be purchased in a single bound volume, but the Bible is actually a library of books. Today, the Protestant Bible is made up of 66 books and includes 10 genres of literature, 185 songs, 1,189 chapters, and 31,102 verses.[2] The Catholic Bible includes 7 additional books, bringing its total to 73, and the Eastern Orthodox Bible adds 5 more for a whopping 78 in total. The Bible is big, messy, and complex. The authors don't always agree with each other, and the stories don't always match up. We do not have a well-behaved Bible. Sadly, many Christians have decided they need to make this wild and wonderful collection of writings behave in ways they find palatable and ideologically advantageous. Not only that, but they've decided the Bible needs to play by our modern rules.

During the Enlightenment, starting in the seventeenth century, reason and logic became the primary ways people in the

2. "The Books of the Bible," Blue Letter Bible, accessed January 8, 2025, https://www.blueletterbible.org/study/misc/66books.cfm.

West understood their world, including religion and faith—previously realms of knowledge governed by faith and church authority. During this time, the scientific method rose to prominence as the way to assess and acquire knowledge. The scientific method goes something like this:

Question > Hypothesis > Testing > Analysis

This method is repeated over and over until the most reasonable answer to a question is made clear.

In the nineteenth century, Enlightenment ideals and the scientific method profoundly reshaped religion, especially Christianity. A hermeneutic of suspicion was applied to many aspects of Christianity, including the divinity of Jesus, the virgin birth, and miracles. New questions arose about the historical accuracy, seeming inconsistencies, scientific validity, and authorship of the Bible. And because of our inability, as modern Westerners, to discuss nuance without dividing into polarized camps, most people took sides. One side claimed that every word in the Bible is literal and without error, while the other side claimed that the Bible is made up, antiquated, and useless. For the last couple centuries, people have felt forced to decide between these two camps.

If those are our only two options, it is significantly harder to prove that every word in the Bible is literal and without error. Consider a passage like Proverbs 26:4–5:

> Do not answer a fool according to his folly,
>   or you yourself will be just like him.
> Answer a fool according to his folly,
>   or he will be wise in his own eyes.

Don't answer a fool in his folly.
Do answer a fool in his folly.

Seems like a contradiction, doesn't it? But before you throw out your Bible, let me ask you a question: What if the problem isn't the Bible? What if the problem is the way we've been taught to read it?

When we break free from the literal/fictional binary, we are better able to engage with verses like these. We can ask questions of the text:

Who wrote this?

What point were they trying to make?

What genre of literature were they using?

For those who haven't thought about literary genres since high school English class, genre is a classification system that groups written works based on their content, form, style, and purpose. In the Bible, the authors' genre choices contribute to the richness and depth of biblical literature, each genre serving unique purposes and conveying different aspects of theological, historical, and moral teachings.

The genre of Proverbs is commonly called "Wisdom literature." Within Wisdom literature, ethics is often situational, meaning sometimes it's wise to answer a fool in his folly—like when your friend is being ignorant and you want to save them from embarrassment—whereas other times it's unwise to answer a fool in his folly—like feeding an internet troll who is just trying to get attention. Understanding author, intent, and genre transforms an apparent contradiction into a nugget of wisdom. Looking for a third way beyond the literal/fictional binary allows us to see the truth beneath the surface.

But these better ways of reading the Bible take work, and that work starts with not asking the Bible to be something it's not. Far too often, we've applied the scientific method to verses completely uninterested in science. We've held passages written thousands of years before the Enlightenment to modern, post-Enlightenment standards. We've treated this ancient, diverse collection of literature like a rule book, a history book, or a scientific textbook tailored to a reader in twenty-first-century America. It's no wonder so many of us struggle with the Bible or have left it behind completely.

Quiet Times and Cities on Fire

Growing up in conservative evangelicalism meant that a core tenet of living out my faith was a "quiet time." This daily ritual of time spent studying the Bible—nighttime is acceptable, but truly committed Christians wake up early and do it in the morning—is all about being inspired by Scripture to live in accordance with God's rules as a person makes their way through each day.

For a while, I used the One Year Bible for my quiet times. This not only allowed me to check my quiet time box each day but also meant that if I was diligent, I would be able to say I had read through the entire Bible in a year. This was a status-enriching achievement in my circles. The One Year Bible conveniently breaks the entirety of Scripture down into 365 chunks designed to be read in fifteen minutes a day. Each daily reading includes portions of the Old Testament, New Testament, Proverbs, and Psalms to provide variety.

As a seventeen-year-old hoping to grow closer to God and get enough encouragement to make it through my senior year with my newfound faith intact, I was absolutely committed to the reading program. Then, a few weeks in, I read the story of Sodom and Gomorrah in Genesis 19. Growing up in church, I'd heard the passage referenced as God's judgment against gay people, but I'd never actually read the story. I was horrified, not just by the destruction of two cities but more specifically by Lot's offer to hand over his two young daughters to a mob of sexually violent men. Lot says, "I have two daughters who have never slept with a man. Let me bring them out to you, and you can do what you like with them" (Gen. 19:8). The story comes full circle. At the end of the chapter, the daughters get their father drunk and have sex with him so they can bear his children: "So both of Lot's daughters became pregnant by their father. The older daughter had a son, and she named him Moab; he is the father of the Moabites of today. The younger daughter also had a son, and she named him Ben-Ammi; he is the father of the Ammonites of today" (19:36–38).

That's it. Those were the last three sentences of the chapter and the final section of my quiet time for the day. I closed my One Year Bible and contemplated how this horrific story could possibly inspire me to "live for Christ" in any meaningful way. As I walked to my first-period class that morning, I decided I would never again open up my One Year Bible.

When the Bible Lets Us Down

I was taught that the Bible is God's Word handed down to us from heaven—perfect truth without any mixture of error and meant to be read literally in every instance. If something doesn't make sense, causes confusion, or provokes outrage (as is the case when many of us read the story of Lot's daughters), it's our problem, not the Bible's. If a passage in Scripture conflicts with modern science, science is wrong, not the Bible. If we have questions or doubts, those are indicative of sin in our lives, not evidence that our biblical interpretation might be off.

When I look back at the parade of expulsions that was my formative years, I realize that questioning prevailing Bible interpretations got me kicked out of a Christian school in fourth grade, a youth group in seventh grade, and a Christian denomination (or two) as an adult. I think the religious leaders in those spaces thought that kicking me out would somehow shut down my questions, that I would be put in my place and finally understand the danger of those questions, but instead they were magnified. They weighed on me. My unanswered questions hung heavy around my neck as if someone had chained dumbbells together and forced me to carry them everywhere I went.

How can a loving God call for the murder of every man, woman, child, and animal in a city like Jericho?

How can a merciful God sentence the vast majority of humans—many of whom have never even heard the name of Jesus—to eternal conscious torment in the fires of hell?

How can a good God tell slaves to obey their masters?

How can a just God prescribe a life of subjugation for women simply because of their gender?

How can a gracious God perpetrate genocide by sending a flood to drown every human on earth except for one family?

How can a kind God call my LGBTQ+ loved ones an abomination?

I tried to find answers to these questions by reading the Bible the way I'd been taught, but it didn't work. No amount of quiet times could quiet my doubts. No amount of church connections could mend my ever-increasing spiritual disconnection.

Peter Enns gives words to my experience when he writes, "The spiritual disconnection many feel today stems precisely from expecting (or being told to expect) the Bible to be holy, perfect, and clear, when in fact after reading it they find it to be morally suspect, out of touch, confusing, and just plain weird."[3]

3. Peter Enns, *How the Bible Actually Works: In Which I Explain How An Ancient, Ambiguous, and Diverse Book Leads Us to Wisdom Rather Than Answers—and Why That's Great News* (HarperOne, 2019), 5.

I was told to read the Bible for inspiration and spiritual nourishment. "It's like food for your soul," I once heard a pastor say. "If you don't eat, your body breaks down. If you don't read your Bible, your soul breaks down."

But it was often the stuff I read in the Bible that broke down my soul. When I read it looking for answers, I emerged with more questions. When I searched it for inspiration, I came away feeling discouraged. I felt like many of my experiences with Scripture were leading me away from the Jesus whose love changed my life and toward a cruel and capricious God who terrified me.

What do we do when the Bible lets us down? In my experience, we usually take a break from reading it. Sometimes that break lasts for a week, and other times it lasts for a lifetime. So that's what I did. I put down my Bible, and I didn't pick it up again for a long time.

When Church Leaves Jesus Behind

Pretty soon my disillusion with the Bible spread to my role at the church as I watched our pastoral leadership weaponize the Scriptures in ways that lent spiritual authority to prejudice, partisan politics, and oppression. They used Bible verses to baptize bigotry.

On my first day on staff, an executive pastor took me on a tour of the facility. It was spread out over a 140-acre campus with a cumulative square footage of over 150,000. This multi-hour tour culminated in the worship center, a trilevel venue that could seat about 7,500 people.

On the tour, the pastor walked me to the highest point in the auditorium. Standing at the top of the balcony, he made a sweeping hand gesture and said, "Zach, you have three things in your life right now: your wife, seminary, and this church. You simply won't have enough time and energy to give all three of them what they need from you. You're going to have to cheat one of them." Then he gave me such an intense look that his face is forever burned into my memory, and he said, "Zach, I don't care which one you cheat, but do not cheat this church."

This church had strict rules about who could lead and who couldn't, with explicit sanctions against women leading and unwritten rules for people of color. LGBTQ+ folks weren't even allowed to be church members, much less on staff. The executive leadership team consisted of uniformly straight, White,[4] politically conservative men.

Our senior pastor was a televangelist and a top Southern Baptist Convention leader, serving as a faith adviser to president Donald Trump. He spent his Sunday morning sermons wielding the Bible like a sword against anyone he didn't like, and the list was long: liberals, progressives, gay people, social justice warriors, Democrats, "baby killers" (people who were pro-choice), immigrants, "thugs" (code for minorities who didn't conform to White cultural norms), feminists, and so on.

I repeatedly saw the Bible weaponized to subjugate women, justify slavery, bash LGBTQ+ folks, cover up abuse, and exclude anyone brave enough to speak out against these injustices. I'm ashamed to admit that early on in my time there, I wielded the Bible in the same way—to great applause from the pastoral staff—but I couldn't keep it up. A combination of my personal

4. I am taking a cue from Love L. Sechrest, New Testament scholar at Columbia Theological Seminary, who recommends capitalizing all racial and ethnic categories: "I capitalize words that refer to subpopulations by race or ethnicity. This practice is ubiquitous in our society when referring to Asian-, Latinx-, Irish-, and Native-Americans, etc. Though contested, we can see it with increasing frequency when using the term 'Black' to refer to African Americans. Less common, however, is my practice of capitalizing 'White' when referring to that group of Americans: To not name 'White' as a race is, in fact, an anti-Black act which frames Whiteness as both neutral and the standard." Sechrest, *Race and Rhyme: Rereading the New Testament*, 77.

struggles with Scripture and my increasing unwillingness to use it to hurt people led me to a tipping point.

I began to ask questions, and they were met with warnings to stay in my place. I started not following directives that I found to be immoral or, in a few cases, illegal. These actions were met with anger. Not long after this transition, an argument with the pastor turned into suspension from work. The morning my suspension ended, I walked into the teaching pastor's office to figure out what to do next. He had prepared a written apology for me in advance. He encouraged me to memorize it and repeat it to the senior pastor as a form of biblical repentance.

I remember it like yesterday, reading that prewritten apology with the words "biblical repentance" echoing in my mind. I remember the way the paper felt in my hands. I remember the heat rising up in my chest and blushing out through my cheeks. Enough was enough. I set the paper down on his desk, told him I couldn't do it anymore, and walked out of his office.

Picking Up the Bible Again

I had become not only one of the twenty-six million people who have stopped reading their Bibles but also one of the millions who have left church behind. Over the last twenty years, church membership has fallen 23 percent, while the number of Americans who do not identify with any religion has ballooned to 21 percent of the population.[5] Why is this happening?

There are many reasons, but I can tell you why I left and why so many of the people I know left: The churches they joined and the leaders they followed weaponized the Bible in ways that hurt them and the people they love. Millions of these

5. Jeffrey M. Jones, "U.S. Church Membership Falls Below Majority for First Time," Gallup, March 29, 2021, https://news.gallup.com/poll/341963/church-membership-falls-below-majority-first-time.aspx.

defectors are not rejecting Jesus; they are rejecting the use of Jesus's name for the purpose of domination and oppression. They aren't rejecting the Bible; they are rejecting harmful ways of reading it.

I'm convinced that this rejection doesn't make them un-Christian. It makes them Christlike. Jesus chastised folks who weaponized Scripture and elevated it above love of neighbor. He repeatedly denounced those who used sacred texts to divide rather than unite, incite violence rather than make peace, and exclude rather than include.

Like so many others, after I put my Bible on the shelf and walked out of the church, I had no idea there was anything other than what I'd left behind. I didn't know there were better ways to read the Bible. I didn't know there were healthier expressions of church. I spent the better part of six months in a deep depression. Since the age of nineteen, my professional life had revolved around being a pastor, and now I was an unemployed seminary student who hated the Bible. I spent most nights during that stretch crying myself to sleep on the couch.

Then I met Pete. Pete was the pastor at a nondenominational church down the road from my apartment. Seeing how I was struggling, one of my seminary professors connected me with Pete because he thought he might be able to help me.

I traded emails with his administrator, and we set up a lunch meeting for the following week. I got there a little early, sat in a booth facing the front of the restaurant, and anxiously watched the door.

A few minutes later, a man who had to be at least six foot five and couldn't have weighed more than 170 pounds walked in. I recognized him from his picture, but I was thrown off by how tall and slender he was. I was wearing a suit, the required uniform at my previous church, while Pete sported jeans and a V-neck T-shirt.

I stood up and waved to him. Pete walked over with the biggest smile on his face and said, "Zach-man! Great to meet you!" And then he bent down and gave me a bear hug. I'm a former college football player, but stretching my arms up to embrace a guy five inches taller than me felt a little bit like hugging my dad when I was a kid.

We sat down, and Pete said, "Why don't you take that suit jacket off? Do you actually like wearing that thing?"

Normally I would have said something like, "It's not too bad," but I already felt so comfortable with him that I replied, "No, man. I hate suits."

With my jacket off and my dress-shirt sleeves rolled up, we sat and ate and talked for almost three hours. Pete had a kindness about him that I'd never experienced in a pastor. He listened to me and asked questions, never once looking past me or checking his phone like he had something more important to do.

He also bought my lunch, which was great because my wife and I had absolutely no money at the time. I had spent the last two years working sixty hours a week for $15,000 a year, and the church (which took in about $70 million per year) had automatically deducted 10 percent of my check as a tithe. My wife, Amy, was in graduate school too. We were taking out extra school loans just to buy groceries.

Pete and I started meeting regularly to talk about life, church, and the Bible. I eventually joined the staff at the church he pastored, and it ended up being our primary sponsor church when we moved back to Austin in 2015 to launch Restore.

As Pete mentored me over the next few years, he regularly did something I'd never experienced before. He encouraged me to ask my questions and voice my doubts. At first, we argued quite a bit. Well, more accurately, I argued and Pete listened. Sure, he engaged and pushed back and made me think, but it was all wrapped in such a compelling kindness.

It was during this time that I picked up my Bible again, but I was still stuck in the old ways of reading it. I brought up all the old interpretations during my conversations with Pete, but he provided a different perspective. During one memorable exchange, I got frustrated and blurted out, "But that's what it says in the Bible! Are you even reading it?"

Pete calmly responded, "Yes, I am. I just think you're reading it wrong."

Could I have been reading it wrong? Could the pastors and teachers I had been trained under have been reading it wrong too? What if the problem wasn't the Bible but the way I'd been taught to read it?

As I began to consider these questions, something started to shift. Like ice thawing in the spring, it happened slowly at first, but I began to realize that even though I believed the Bible was inspired by God, the interpretations I'd been given were not.

Pete was one of my first teachers on this journey of finding better ways to read the Bible, but he was far from my last. I have been transformed by the writing of people like James Cone, Rachel Held Evans, bell hooks, Gustavo Gutiérrez, Howard Thurman, Lisa Sharon Harper, Kaitlin Curtice, Jonathan Merritt, Danya Ruttenberg, David Gushee, Trey Ferguson, Leonardo Boff, Wendell Berry, Sarah Bessey, Kathy Khang, Charles Marsh, Father Greg Boyle, Anne Lamott, Mark Charles, Brennan Manning, and James Baldwin. I model my justice work after the activism of people like Fannie Lou Hamer, Cesar Chavez, Dorothy Day, Mitsuye Endo, Latasha Morrison, Frederick Douglass, Dietrich Bonhoeffer, Shane Claiborne, Carlos Rodriguez, Bree Newsome Bass, Sojourner Truth, Bobby Kennedy, and Dolores Huerta. I have learned so much from the scholarship of people like Angela Parker, Walter Brueggemann, Karen Keen, Amy-Jill Levine, Willie James Jennings, Ellen Davis, N. T. Wright, Love Sechrest, Diana Butler Bass, Jemar Tisby, Wilda Gafney, Austen

Hartke, Stanley Hauerwas, Shai Held, Kristin Kobes Du Mez, David Bentley Hart, Reinhold Niebuhr, Samuel Perry, Billie Hoard, Andrew Whitehead, Beth Allison Barr, Scot McKnight, Justo González, Judy Fentress-Williams, and Peter Enns. And I continue to be inspired by the preaching of people like Martin Luther King Jr., Nadia Bolz-Weber, William J. Barber II, Sally Gary, Óscar Romero, George MacDonald, Paula Williams, Beth Moore, Gail Song Bantum, Brian Zahnd, and Barbara Brown Taylor.

We'll hear from several of these writers and thinkers throughout this book. I hope they are as helpful on your journey as they have been on mine.

The prophet Isaiah looked forward to a time when God would make all things right again. No more pain, no more sorrow, no more violence. To accomplish this restoration, people would "beat their swords into plowshares and their spears into pruning hooks" (Isa. 2:4). In other words, making things right includes transforming weapons of harm into tools of healing. I believe this will happen in complete fullness someday, but we don't have to wait for that day to come before we start dismantling our weapons. As the apostle Paul says, "Today is the day of salvation" (2 Cor. 6:2 NLT).

Today is the day of being set free from everything that gets in the way of our flourishing and the flourishing of our neighbors. Today is the day to start leaving behind bad Bible interpretations and choosing to read Scripture in ways that lead to healing, wholeness, and fullness of life.

2

some lenses are better than others

> You don't have a "biblical worldview." You have a worldview shaped by your subculture's interpretation of Christianity. . . . Admit influences; purge bad ones; change systems.
>
> —Samuel Perry

My seminary degree was a 120-hour master's program dedicated to the study of every chapter of the Bible. If you know anything about seminary, you know it involves a ton of reading; we were often required to read five books for a single class. In the forty classes I took, 97 percent of the books assigned were written by straight, White men. If you struggle with math like I do, that's a grand total of six books out of about two hundred that were written by women or people of color, and none by LGBTQ+ folks.

One professor, introducing a book by Cuban American church historian Justo González, told us to keep in mind that it was written by a Latino theologian and so probably was biased. Of course, we never heard that the books from men of European descent might also contain biases. Maybe because thirty-nine of my forty seminary classes were taught by White men.

Regardless of our racial or cultural heritage, we all have biases—lenses through which we interpret the Bible. That's not the problem. The problem is pretending that one group of people doesn't bring any biases to their Scripture reading while everyone else does.

Many theological bookstores and libraries have sections for "Black theology," "feminist theology," "Latino/a theology," "queer theology," "disabled theology," and so on.[1] There aren't sections called "White theology" or "straight theology" or "masculine theology," however. The perspective of a straight, White, able-bodied man is assumed to be normative; everything else needs a disclaimer.

Historically, this posture is incredibly common among men of European descent. The assumption is that we are objective and everyone else is aberrant; we are reading the Bible without bias and everyone else is letting their biases get in the way.

For most of my life, I rarely thought about being White or male or heterosexual or cisgender or able-bodied or American or middle class. I was conditioned to believe that all those characteristics were normal and anything else was abnormal. Because of this, I also believed I didn't have any lenses when I interpreted the Bible. In fact, I didn't think I was interpreting it at all; I thought I was just learning and teaching the plain meaning of Scripture.

But the truth is that the folks most capable of understanding the "plain meaning of Scripture" by just reading or hearing it are ancient Israelites or first-century Near Easterners living under Roman occupation—and even they debated the various texts. We

1. It's important to note that some scholars have pioneered these disciplines for the very purpose of differentiating them from Eurocentric theological streams, proudly claiming the labels.

are all interpreting. We make interpretive decisions without even realizing it, based on a combination of who we are, what we've been taught, where we grew up, and how we see the world. We don't intrinsically understand the contexts and cultures of the biblical texts, and we don't natively speak Hebrew or Greek or Aramaic. We read Scripture over the shoulders of those who originally received it, which means the very first thing we need to do when trying to understand the Bible is to practice some humility.

Is Our Good News Actually Good?

About halfway through seminary, I was humbled. It happened one day when I was in the office at the megachurch I worked for. We rotated through "pastors on call" each day—staff members who handled walk-ins requesting someone to talk or pray with. I was just an intern, but the pastor on call that day was preoccupied with his lunch meeting, so he told me to serve in his place.

I walked down the stairs and found a Black man waiting for me. In a thick accent I couldn't quite place, he told me his name was Junior. He'd immigrated to the United States from Haiti the year before, following the devastating earthquake of 2010, in which he'd lost everything. He told me about how things had only gotten worse over the last year—so bad, in fact, that he was contemplating suicide.

This felt like one of those moments I'd been trained for in evangelism classes. I asked Junior if he'd ever heard of the gospel. He said no. I knew this was it. I was going to lead Junior to Christ, and that pastor who couldn't leave his BLT sandwich to pray with someone was going to be so proud of me.

I began to walk Junior down the Romans Road, a popular evangelistic tool. I started with the bad news. "Romans 3:23 says, 'All have sinned and fall short of the glory of God,' and Romans 6:23 says, 'The wages of sin is death.'" Then I hit him with the good news. "But Romans 6:23 doesn't stop there. Paul goes on to say that 'the gift of God is eternal life in Christ Jesus our Lord.'"

When I was in college, I participated in evangelism training at the church where I worked. The theme of the training was "Fishers of Men," and there were three stations:

1. "Going Out on the Boat"—What do we need to pack? How do we prepare? What do we wear?
2. "Baiting and Casting"—What kind of bait should we use given the type of person we're talking to?
3. "Reeling Them In"—How do we "set the hook"? How do we make sure the evangelism conversation ends with praying the prayer of salvation?

In that conversation with Junior, I knew all I had to do was set the hook and reel him in. "Would you like to pray and ask Jesus to come into your heart?" I inquired earnestly. Junior stared at me blankly. Uh-oh, I thought. Why wasn't he already fully immersed in the baptismal waters by now? Had I gone too fast? Not quoted enough Scripture?

Finally, he said, "What did you call all of this? The 'gospel' or something?"

"Yes, this is the gospel."

"What does 'gospel' mean?"

"Good news," I replied.

"Good news about what?"

My heart started pounding. Had I skipped that part in my haste to have Junior repeat the sinner's prayer after me? "I don't think you understand," I stammered. "Let me explain it again. The good news of Jesus Christ starts in Romans 3:23, where it says, 'All have sinned and fall short . . .'"

"No, you don't understand!" Junior cut me off. "How is any of this 'good news' for me? Will it bring my home back from the rubble? Will it keep my father alive? Will it buy food for my wife and children?"

They hadn't covered any of this in the "Fishers of Men" training. "Well, no," I said, beads of sweat starting to form around my collar. "But it does mean you can go to heaven instead of hell when you die!"

"Who cares about that? My life is hell right now," Junior said as he put his head in his hands.

Throughout my life, I'd been told that the gospel of Jesus Christ is meant to give us hope for life after death, but what about life before death? Is there any good news for us right now? Is there good news for someone like Junior?

In her book *The Very Good Gospel*, Lisa Sharon Harper writes, "If one's gospel falls mute when facing people who need good news the most—the impoverished, the oppressed, and the broken—then it's no good news at all."[2]

Junior and I ended up talking for an hour that day and then we met up again the next day. Quickly, we became close friends—sharing many meals together and spending time in each other's homes. Over the next few years of friendship, Junior taught me more about the gospel than any Bible professor ever had. He helped me take off my lenses and see things from his perspective. During that time, through the work of Jesus and incredible mentors like Junior, it became glaringly apparent that I had a serious problem when it came to the Bible.

"I Have a Problem with the Bible"

I am a White, heterosexual, cisgender, able-bodied man. I was born into a Christian, middle-class, two-parent family in the United States. If I were to take a privilege test, I could check

2. Lisa Sharon Harper, *The Very Good Gospel: How Everything Wrong Can Be Made Right* (WaterBrook, 2016), 14.

every box; if the Western church had a caste system, I would be at the top.

Do these uncontrollable characteristics make me an inherently bad or oppressive person? No. But they do drastically affect the way I interpret the Bible.

Brian Zahnd puts it like this: "I have a problem with the Bible. Here's my problem . . . I'm an ancient Egyptian. I'm a comfortable Babylonian. I'm a Roman in his villa. That's my problem. See, I'm trying to read the Bible for all it's worth, but I'm not a Hebrew slave suffering in Egypt. I'm not a conquered Judean deported to Babylon. I'm not a first century Jew living under Roman occupation. I'm a citizen of a superpower. I was born among the conquerors. I live in the empire."[3]

Erna Kim Hackett calls this problem "Disney princess theology." She writes,

> As each individual reads Scripture, they see themselves as the princess in every story. They are Esther, never Xerxes or Haman. They are Peter, but never Judas. They are the woman anointing Jesus, never the Pharisees. They are the Jews escaping slavery, never Egypt. For citizens of the most powerful country in the world, who enslaved both Native and Black people, to see itself as Israel and not Egypt when studying Scripture is a perfect example of Disney princess theology. And it means that as people in power, they have no lens for locating themselves rightly in Scripture or society—and it has made them blind and utterly ill-equipped to engage issues of power and injustice. It is some very weak Bible work.[4]

3. Brian Zahnd, "My Problem with the Bible," *Brian Zahnd* (blog), February 17, 2014, https://brianzahnd.com/2014/02/problem-bible.

4. Erna Kim Hackett, "Why I Stopped Talking About Racial Reconciliation and Started Talking About White Supremacy," *Inheritance*, March 25, 2020, https://www.inheritancemag.com/stories/why-i-stopped-talking-about-racial-reconciliation-and-started-talking-about-white-supremacy.

The point is true for all of us to some extent. We are not the original audience for which Scripture was written. We all come to the biblical text with biases. We all interpret through lenses.

When I began to realize this truth, I decided to take off all my lenses. I wanted to make sure I wasn't bringing any interpretive bias to the Bible. I was determined to read it objectively. That lasted for about a week, because it quickly became obvious that removing all my lenses was impossible. None of us are truly objective because none of us can remove who we are, what we've been through, where we grew up, or our various underlying assumptions when we read the Bible.

Applying our unique experiences and perspectives to Scripture isn't a bad thing in and of itself, as reading the Bible in healthy and diverse communities helps the text come alive in amazing ways. But we all have to be aware of what we're bringing to the table. The Bible doesn't interpret itself.

I still have the Introduction to Systematic Theology class notes from my first semester of seminary. On February 8, 2011, as I furiously scribbled notes under fluorescent lights at one of the most rigorously conservative seminaries in America, my professor read a quote from the book *How to Think Theologically*: "The biblical text does not speak for itself; every reading is someone's interpretation of it."[5]

I was both shocked and grateful when I came upon this quote in my notes years later. Just reading the Bible is an act of interpretation rendered through our lenses. My professor said the practice of biblical interpretation is called "exegesis" and that we'd be learning how to exegete Scripture throughout the rest of our time in seminary. A young man raised his hand and

5. Howard W. Stone and James O. Duke, *How to Think Theologically*, 3rd ed. (Fortress, 2013), 49.

asked, "Will we learn how to do pure exegesis so we know that our interpretation is correct?"

My professor responded abruptly and directly, "Pure exegesis is impossible. Every reading of the Scripture is an interpretation of the Scripture."

No one "just reads the Bible." That statement is not "conservative" or "progressive" but the truth. I slowly but surely began to realize that, even though we can't remove all our lenses and come to the Bible with objectivity, we can choose which lenses we put on when interpreting Scripture. Kelly Brown Douglas, a theologian and Episcopal priest, puts it like this: "No theology emerges in a social, historical or cultural vacuum, and neither does any particular interpretation or approach to Scripture. Both theological and biblical discourse is shaped by the complicated historical realities of the persons conducting them."[6]

This realization started a journey for me of trying on dozens of lenses and humbly asking Jesus to lead me to the most Christlike combination. It was like getting a vision test at the eye doctor, like having that machine put in front of you as the optometrist flips the lenses and asks, "1 or 2?" testing different combinations to see which one provides the clearest image. The first step is recognizing which lenses we're wearing and then determining whether they're harmful or healthy, whether they're Christlike or un-Christlike. Because the truth is, some lenses are better than others.

6. Kelly Brown Douglas, "Marginalized People, Liberating Perspectives: A Womanist Approach to Biblical Interpretation," *Anglican Theological Review* 83, no. 1 (Winter 2001): 41.

part 2

lenses that inflict harm

3

the literalism lens

"The Bible Says It, I Believe It, That Settles It"

> Biblical literalism has never been about being faithful to the Bible, but about weaponizing selective parts of the Bible to give a personally preferred interpretative outcome the weight of God's full authority.
>
> —David Simmons

Growing up in the Southern Baptist Convention, a denomination generally uncomfortable with anything charismatic or overtly spiritual, I was taught a classical view of the Trinity: Father, Son, and Holy Spirit. For all intents and purposes, however, the Trinity was more like Father, Son, and Holy Bible. That is, the faith communities in which I was raised treated the Bible like it was divinely handed down to us mapped and wrapped in the same leather-bound form that Bible college grads receive with their names etched in gold across the front.

"The Bible says it, I believe it, that settles it" was a common refrain from the pulpits of my childhood. Pastors often claimed to be reading the Bible literally without any interpretation or bias. Anything else was an attack on something called "inerrancy." If you grew up in more conservative branches of Christianity, like I did, chances are you've heard about inerrancy.

But the doctrine of inerrancy is a relatively new invention, formulated in the nineteenth century by protofundamentalist scholars B. B. Warfield and Charles Hodge and codified in the 1978 Chicago Statement on Biblical Inerrancy. The second paragraph of the statement opens with these words: "The following Statement affirms this inerrancy of Scripture afresh, making clear our understanding of it and warning against its denial. We are persuaded that to deny it is to set aside the witness of Jesus Christ and of the Holy Spirit and to refuse that submission to the claims of God's own Word which marks true Christian faith."[1]

In other words, according to the writers and signers of this statement (notable among them are slavery apologist John MacArthur,[2] sexual abuser Paul Pressler,[3] and disgraced Southwestern Seminary president Paige Patterson[4]), denying their definition of biblical inerrancy is akin to denying Christ. They explicitly claim that anyone who doesn't adhere to their

1. International Council on Biblical Inerrancy, *The Chicago Statement on Biblical Inerrancy* (International Council on Biblical Inerrancy, 1978), 1, available at https://library.dts.edu/Pages/TL/Special/ICBI_1.pdf.

2. Rick Pidcock, "What Has John MacArthur Actually Said About Race, Slavery and the Curse of Ham?," *Baptist News*, June 20, 2022, https://baptistnews.com/article/what-has-john-macarthur-actually-said-about-race-slavery-and-the-curse-of-ham.

3. Bob Smietana, "A Southern Baptist Leader Hid Decades of Abuse: Will His Fall Doom SBC Abuse Reforms?," *Religion News*, January 22, 2024, https://religionnews.com/2024/01/22/a-southern-baptist-leader-used-religion-and-piety-to-mask-decades-of-abuse-will-his-fall-doom-sbc-abuse-reforms.

4. Kate Shellnutt, "Paige Patterson Fired by Southwestern, Stripped of Retirement Benefits," *Christianity Today*, May 30, 2018, https://www.christianitytoday.com/news/2018/may/paige-patterson-fired-southwestern-baptist-seminary-sbc.html.

understanding of the Bible has walked away from the Christian faith.

The 1978 Chicago Statement on Biblical Inerrancy is one of three statements adopted by this same group. The Chicago Statement on Biblical Hermeneutics (1982) and the Chicago Statement on Biblical Application (1986) make it clear that disagreeing with any of their biblical interpretations equates to apostasy. In the preamble to the Chicago Statement on Biblical Hermeneutics, the authors write, "While we recognize that belief in the inerrancy of Scripture is basic to maintaining its authority, the values of that commitment are only as real as one's understanding of the meaning of Scripture."[5]

Taken together, the Chicago statements teach that someone's Christian faith is only as true as their commitment to inerrancy, and their inerrancy is only as good as their commitment to the biblical interpretations promoted by the statement's authors. These interpretations include everything from the authority of Scripture over scientific discovery to prescriptions for marriage and divorce to an endorsement of just war theory.

The Bible in Black and White

Of the 334 original signers of the Chicago statements, only 11 (3 percent) were not White men. This means that the statements do not attempt to coalesce the varied opinions on biblical interpretation throughout church history; rather, they attempt to canonize the interpretations of White, conservative, evangelical, Protestant men and then pass them off as final and authoritative.

In her excellent book *If God Still Breathes, Why Can't I?*, New Testament scholar Angela Parker puts it like this: "White male

5. International Council on Biblical Inerrancy, preamble to *Chicago Statement on Biblical Hermeneutics* (International Council on Biblical Inerrancy, 1982), available at https://library.dts.edu/Pages/TL/Special/ICBI_2.pdf.

biblical scholars have outlined inerrancy and infallibility in such a way that anyone who questions or pushes back against these accepted viewpoints becomes disciplined and subsequently ostracized."[6]

You may have heard preachers use the doctrine of inerrancy or the lens of literalism like this before. One of the pastors I listened to in college frequently said that if people didn't agree with something he was teaching, the problem was not with him but with the God who wrote the Bible. "I'm just telling you what it says in black and white," he would often say.

Equating a pastor's interpretation with God's truth assumes that questioning the pastor is the same as questioning God. The problem isn't believing the Bible is inspired by God;[7] the problem is equating someone's interpretation with God's inspiration.

One of the most prominent biblical battlegrounds for these inerrancy litmus tests is the first few chapters of Genesis. The Chicago Statement on Biblical Hermeneutics devotes an article to a literalistic interpretation of Genesis 1–11. This statement may be from the early 1980s, but using a literalistic interpretation of Genesis as a litmus test for true faith is nothing new.

During the seventeenth century, the Catholic Church put scientists on trial who posited theories that "contradicted Scripture" and were thus labeled as heretics. During these trials, Galileo was found to be guilty of heresy for claiming that he had made groundbreaking observations that the earth revolved

6. Angela N. Parker, *If God Still Breathes, Why Can't I? Black Lives Matter and Biblical Authority* (Eerdmans, 2021), 48–49.

7. People mean many different things when they say the Bible is "inspired by God." Karen Keen has a wonderful explanation of the six most common views on inspiration in chaps. 5–6 of her book *The Word of a Humble God*. I appreciate Keen's definition of inspiration when she writes, "The Bible is a product of God's humility in sharing power with human beings. It reflects God-given human agency in collaboration with the Creator." Keen, *The Word of a Humble God: The Origins, Inspiration, and Interpretation of Scripture* (Eerdmans, 2022), 118.

around the sun instead of vice versa. He was found guilty of heresy and spent the last decade of his life under house arrest. Another cosmological theorist named Giordano Bruno was brought to trial under the Roman Inquisition for his beliefs about the possibility of life on other planets as well as theological opinions that departed from those of the Catholic Church. He was found guilty of heresy and burned at the stake.

These examples may seem extreme, but the pain caused by literalistic understandings of Genesis are not confined to the past. I've talked with hundreds of people over the years who left Christianity because of literalistic interpretations of Genesis's stories. I've also talked with people who are still hanging on to faith but have been deeply wounded by church leaders who say that one must believe in a seven-day creation in order to be a faithful Christian.

I need to add something important here. I honestly don't care if you believe the earth is six thousand or six billion years old. I don't care if you believe Adam and Eve were literal people or if you think of them as characters in a mythological story. What I'm concerned about is making matters on which faithful Christians disagree into a litmus test for true Christianity. This practice not only has been incredibly damaging to people but also has nothing to do with what the biblical authors are trying to communicate.

There is a temptation on the other side as well. Our twenty-first-century Western inclination is to say, "If every word isn't literal, then it's all a lie. If it isn't historically accurate, then we can't trust it and we should throw it all away." One side says, "It has to be 100 percent literal, historical, and scientific," while the other side says, "Throw it out, because it's all made up."

But when it comes to understanding the stories from Genesis, we do not have to choose between a literalistic interpretation and a fictional one. I firmly believe that both ends of the spectrum are ultimately unhelpful when trying to decipher the truths found in this portion of Scripture.

Old Testament scholar Daniel Lowery puts it like this: "These stories were true to their original audience and have truths that carry forward to today, but they may not be 'true' in the twenty-first-century Western way we often define that term—which is usually 'provable scientifically.' We usually define 'true' as literal, but that's a relatively new phenomenon."[8]

"True" equating to "literal" is not only relatively new but also an unhelpful paradigm when trying to interpret Scripture. Albert Wolters, a professor, scholar, and expert on Genesis, has studied some of the oldest versions of the Bible that we have (the Dead Sea Scrolls) and has written some of the most influential work defending the validity of the Bible, especially Genesis. He states very simply, "Figurative language is not necessarily a second-best way of conveying truth; in some cases it is far more straightforward and effective than any other way of reporting facts. Perhaps the early history of the world as recorded in Scripture is such a case."[9]

"True" Stories

We often learn truth not from a formal recitation of facts but from the stories we live and share. When my kids were younger, they would ask me to tell them stories at the most random times. If you've spent time around kids, you know what I'm talking about. Before bed, in the car, while eating dinner, when they're bored sitting on the toilet—it doesn't matter. When the mood strikes them, you better have a story ready.

Early on I would crack under pressure, failing to think of any good stories, but then I came up with a parenting hack: I

8. Daniel Lowery, personal communication with author, May 12, 2022.
9. A. M. Wolters, "Thoughts on Genesis," *Calvinist Contact* (1990): 5.

created my own fictional universe that served as a setting and provided characters for every story. I didn't come up with it out of thin air. It was a strange mash-up of Star Wars and Peter Rabbit, but it worked.

Every time my boys wanted to hear a story, I would start by saying, "A long time ago in a burrow far, far away, there lived a little bunny rabbit named Cuppy." I would then tell a story about Cuppy the rabbit going on an adventure, running into some trouble, usually caused by his own mischievous personality, and then ultimately triumphing.

I began to use these stories to teach my boys life lessons, usually conveying a central theme that there are no "bad guys," just people who have been hurt and, because they've never healed, end up hurting others.

One story was about a fox named Maverick (I know, now I'm mixing in *Top Gun*), who steals Cuppy's soccer ball while Cuppy and his friends are playing. After finally tracking down Maverick and getting his ball back, Cuppy asks him why he stole the soccer ball. Maverick says, "I don't have any friends and no one ever wants to play with me, so I thought if I stole your ball you would have to play with me." Cuppy invites Maverick to play with them, and they all become friends. The end.

A few weeks after I told that story, one of my kids came home from school and said, "I met a kid like Maverick on the playground today." At first I didn't realize what he was talking about, but then he reminded me of the Cuppy story. The boy on the playground was disrupting everything a group of boys, including my son, was trying to play. A few of the kids got understandably mad and told the disruptive boy to go away. But it kept happening.

"Then I remembered the story!" my son said. And so he asked the disruptive kid if he wanted to play with the group, and the kid immediately joined in. My son finished his report by proudly stating, "And now we are all friends, just like Cuppy and Maverick!"

Let me ask you something: Is the story about Cuppy and Maverick true?

Is it literal or historical? Obviously not. But is it true? Absolutely. And that truth stuck with my son.

If I had read my kids studies and data about why bullies act out, do you think that truth would have sunk in? Of course not. But the story of Cuppy and Maverick not only stuck with them; it also changed how they viewed the world and the way they interacted with others.

That story wasn't literal, but it was true, and that's because narrative storytelling and figurative language are not inferior ways of portraying truth. Many times they are more effective for our spiritual formation than a recitation of facts.

If you have any doubt about that, look no further than Jesus.

Jesus the Storyteller

The Gospels (the books of Matthew, Mark, Luke, and John) record the life of Jesus, especially his last three years on earth. During that time, whether addressing twenty thousand people on a hillside or his twelve disciples around a fire, Jesus was constantly teaching. Sometimes his lessons were literal and straightforward: "Love your neighbor as yourself" (Mark 12:31) or "Do to others as you would have them do to you" (Luke 6:31). But other times Jesus used figurative language. In fact, Jesus's most frequently used teaching method was telling stories, commonly referred to as parables.

Jesus tells a parable forty-one times in the Gospel accounts. In fact, Mark describes his teaching this way: "Jesus used many similar stories and illustrations to teach the people as much as they could understand. In fact, in his public ministry he never taught without using parables" (Mark 4:33–34 NLT). These parables weren't a precise recitation of historical or scientific facts, but they conveyed vital truths about who God is and who we are. Again, I'm not saying that you have to believe that all the people and events in these stories are fictitious; rather, I'm saying that the biblical authors weren't working from the literal-versus-fictional binary that many of us bring to the text.

The biblical authors were not concerned with history or science in the way we conceptualize them. They were concerned with conveying the truth about who God is, who we are, and how we are supposed to live in this world. Jesus's parables are one of many examples of God communicating with humanity in ways that we can wrap our minds around.

I love the way Rachel Held Evans puts it:

> There's a curious but popular notion circulating around the church these days that says God would never stoop to using ancient genre categories to communicate. Speaking to ancient people using their own language, literary structures, and cosmological assumptions would be beneath God, it is said, for only our modern categories of science and history can convey the truth in any meaningful way. In addition to once again prioritizing modern, Western (and often uniquely American) concerns, this notion overlooks one of the most central themes of Scripture itself: God stoops.
>
> From walking with Adam and Eve through the garden of Eden, to traveling with the liberated Hebrew slaves in a pillar of cloud and fire, to slipping into flesh and eating, laughing, suffering, healing, weeping, and dying among us as part of humanity, the God of Scripture stoops and stoops and stoops.
>
> At the heart of the gospel message is the story of a God who stoops to the point of death on a cross. . . . It is no more beneath God to speak to us using poetry, proverb, letters, and legend than

> it is for a mother to read storybooks to her daughter at bedtime. This is who God is. This is what God does.[10]

Our God stoops to be with us. Time and time again, God comes down to us because we can't possibly reach up to him. God condescends to humanity's ways because we can't comprehend his ways. One of the most beautiful pictures of God stooping down to be with us is found in the story of Adam and Eve.

Literalism and Genesis 1–3

The literalism lens usually entails asking questions of and about Scripture that the biblical authors were not trying to answer. This is exactly what we've done with the early chapters of Genesis over the last few hundred years. We've asked questions like these:

> How old is the earth?
> How long did it take God to create the world?
> Where is the garden of Eden?
> Is evolution real?
> When did dinosaurs live?

These questions matter and are worth talking about, but here is what I desperately want us to understand: Genesis 1–3 is not trying to answer any of these questions, because Genesis is not a textbook. Even if we completely disregard evidence from the fossil record, evolutionary theory, and carbon dating, all we have to do is look at Scripture itself to see that it makes no attempt to give a scientific recounting of the earth's origins.

10. Rachel Held Evans, *Inspired: Slaying Giants, Walking on Water, and Loving the Bible Again* (Thomas Nelson, 2018), 11.

For example, after recounting each of the first three creation days, the author of Genesis concludes with the phrase "There was evening, and there was morning . . ." (Gen. 1:5, 8, 13). But look how the fourth day begins: "And God said, 'Let there be lights in the vault of the sky to separate the day from the night, and let them serve as signs to mark sacred times, and days and years'" (1:14). The lights that serve to mark days aren't created until day 4. How could there be "evening and morning" on days 1 through 3 without the sun, moon, and stars?

Another example is found in the order of creation described in Genesis 1 versus Genesis 2. Let's look first at Genesis 1, starting at verse 11:

> Then God said, "Let the land produce vegetation: seed-bearing plants and trees on the land that bear fruit with seed in it, according to their various kinds." And it was so. The land produced vegetation: plants bearing seed according to their kinds and trees bearing fruit with seed in it according to their kinds. And God saw that it was good. And there was evening, and there was morning—the third day. (1:11–13)

Now let's look at Genesis 2, starting at verse 5:

> Now no shrub had yet appeared on the earth and no plant had yet sprung up, for the Lord God had not sent rain on the earth and there was no one to work the ground, but streams came up from the earth and watered the whole surface of the ground. Then the Lord God formed a man from the dust of the ground and breathed into his nostrils the breath of life, and the man became a living being. (2:5–7)

In Genesis 2, God creates man before any shrub or plant appears, but in Genesis 1, the plants are created on day 3 and humanity isn't created until day 6.

These are just two of many examples in Genesis 1–3 showing that the author was not trying to be scientific or literalistic. I'm far from the first person to point out these things. We have recorded evidence of people asking hard questions about Genesis all the way back to Jewish scholars two hundred years before the birth of Jesus. The creation story is interested in something greater and more central to our existence than a play-by-play retelling of terrestrial formation.

Old Testament scholar Peter Enns says, "It is a fundamental misunderstanding of Genesis to expect it to answer questions generated by a modern worldview, such as whether the days were literal or figurative, or whether the days of creation can be lined up with modern science, or whether the flood was local or universal. The question that Genesis is prepared to answer is whether Yahweh, the God of Israel, is worthy of worship."[11]

Not only are we asking Genesis 1–3 questions that it's not interested in answering, we also have so plucked it out of its context, ignored its genre, and applied modern expectations to it that we have completely missed the point. In short, the literalism lens has killed our ability to experience the life-giving beauty of this story. To borrow a line from another pastor, "In the beginning, we misunderstood."[12]

When we remove the literalism lens from our reading of Genesis 1–3—meaning we stop asking it to be a scientifically or historically accurate recounting of the earth's creation—the deeper truth of the story really comes alive: We begin to see it as a portrait of God's majesty, an explanation of God's purpose for the world, and a beautiful picture of God's great love for humanity.

11. Peter Enns, *Inspiration and Incarnation: Evangelicals and the Problem of the Old Testament* (Baker Academic, 2005), 55.

12. Johnny V. Green and John H. Walton, *In the Beginning, We Misunderstood: Interpreting Genesis 1 in Its Original Context* (Baker Books, 2012).

Other Origin Stories

The first thing we have to understand about Genesis 1–3 is that it was not written in a vacuum; it was written in response to origin stories from neighboring nations in order to differentiate the Hebrew God, Yahweh, from the pantheon of gods in the ancient Near East.

One of these stories is called the Enuma Elish, an ancient Babylonian creation myth. This epic poem describes a group of celestial beings establishing the world, ordering the cosmos, and creating humanity. In one section, the god Ea proposes creating humanity to relieve the lesser gods of their labor: "Let me put blood together, and make bones too. Let me set up primeval man: Man shall be his name. Let me create primeval man. The work of the gods shall be imposed on him and so they shall be at leisure. . . . He created mankind from his blood, imposed the toil of the gods on man and released the gods from it."[13]

Another rival origin story is called the Atrahasis Epic, an ancient Mesopotamian recounting of the creation of humanity, the great flood, and various attempts to solve the overpopulation of humans. This epic predates the Enuma Elish but offers a similar perspective on creation and the purpose of humanity. It reads in part, "Great indeed was the drudgery of the gods, the forced labor was heavy, the misery too much. 'Let the midwife create a human being! Let man assume the drudgery of the gods.' They summoned and asked the goddess / the midwife of the gods, wise Mami: 'Will you be the birth goddess, creator of mankind? Create a human being, that he bear the yoke, let man assume the drudgery of the gods.' Mami said: 'I have done away with your heavy labor, I have imposed your drudgery on man.'"[14]

13. Enuma Elish, in *Myths from Mesopotamia: Creation, The Flood, Gilgamesh, and Others*, trans. and ed. Stephanie Dalley (Oxford University Press, 1998), 260–61.
14. Atrahasis, in Dalley, *Myths from Mesopotamia*, 9–11.

Both the Enuma Elish and the Atrahasis Epic predate the Genesis creation story by at least five hundred years. In these stories, as well as the vast majority of other ancient Near Eastern creation myths, humanity is created to make life easier for the gods. Our purpose is to "assume the drudgery of the gods," to bear their yoke, and to carry their burdens.

But the Hebrew people—and now Christians by extension—believe something wholly different. While Genesis 1–3 is similar to other contemporaneous creation myths in many ways, the purpose of humanity's creation is radically different. Here is what the author says:

> Then God said, "Let us make mankind in our image, in our likeness, so that they may rule over the fish in the sea and the birds in the sky, over the livestock and all the wild animals, and over all the creatures that move along the ground." So God created mankind in his own image, in the image of God he created them; male and female he created them. God blessed them and said to them, "Be fruitful and increase in number; fill the earth and subdue it. Rule over the fish in the sea and the birds in the sky and over every living creature that moves on the ground."
>
> Then God said, "I give you every seed-bearing plant on the face of the whole earth and every tree that has fruit with seed in it. They will be yours for food. And to all the beasts of the earth and all the birds in the sky and all the creatures that move along the ground—everything that has the breath of life in it—I give every green plant for food." And it was so.
>
> God saw all that he had made, and it was very good. (1:26–31)

Do you see the stark contrast?

- Other gods create humanity as their property; our God creates humanity in his image and likeness.

- Other gods create humanity as their subservient slaves; our God creates humanity as his representatives on earth and calls us his children.
- Other gods create humanity for the purpose of loading us down with menial work; our God creates humanity for the purpose of partnering with him in the work of helping all things flourish.

These stories became such foundational truths for the Hebrew people that Jesus even drew on their language centuries later. Remember, the Atrahasis Epic says, "Create a human being, that he bear the yoke, let man assume the drudgery of the gods. . . . I have done away with your heavy labor, I have imposed your drudgery on man."[15] But Jesus says, "Come to me, all you who are weary and burdened, and I will give you rest. Take my yoke upon you and learn from me, for I am gentle and humble in heart, and you will find rest for your souls. For my yoke is easy and my burden is light" (Matt. 11:28–30).

Other gods say, "Take our heavy burdens so we can rest," but Jesus says, "Give me your heavy burdens so you can rest." Other gods say, "Take this yoke, because it's hard to bear," but Jesus says, "Take my yoke, because it's easy to bear."

If you've heard this story from Genesis 1–3 before, you know that humans fail to assume the identity and purpose God intends for them. After being tempted by an evil serpent, Adam and Eve choose to turn their backs on God's way and go their own way. This action brings sin and all its side effects into the garden of Eden. As a result, Adam and Eve begin to experience shame, fear, and selfishness for the very first time. Sin also brings a curse that illustrates the ongoing fracture of relationships between God and humanity, between humanity and creation, and within humanity itself.

15. Atrahasis, in Dalley, *Myths from Mesopotamia*, 9.

In the ancient Near East, the prevailing understanding of how the gods reacted when humanity stepped out of line was violent and retributive. If a human disobeyed a god, they were almost always killed. But how does God react when Adam and Eve choose to turn their backs on him and, through their disobedience, break the very good world God created? The answer to this question is the foundational truth of this story.

Seeing God's Character Without a Distorted Lens

Interpreting Genesis 1–3 without the literalism lens reveals God's character in a way that focusing on the earth's age or the historical Adam often obstructs. God's reaction to Adam and Eve's sin in this story illustrates three truths about God's nature.

To see the first element of God's character revealed in this story, we have to backtrack to Genesis 2 for a moment:

> The Lord God made all kinds of trees grow out of the ground—trees that were pleasing to the eye and good for food. In the middle of the garden were the tree of life and the tree of the knowledge of good and evil. . . . The Lord God took the man and put him in the Garden of Eden to work it and take care of it. And the Lord God commanded the man, "You are free to eat from any tree in the garden; but you must not eat from the tree of the knowledge of good and evil, for when you eat from it you will certainly die." (2:9, 15–17)

What does God say will happen if they eat from the tree of the knowledge of good and evil? They will die.

Not long after God says this, Adam and Eve eat from the tree, and what happens? They don't immediately die.

Some argue that Adam and Eve *began* to die that day or that they spiritually died, but the original audience would have understood these verses to mean immediate physical death upon breaking God's rule—because that's what happened when a human disobeyed every other god.

But not this God. God says they will die, but they keep living, albeit now with toil, suffering, and eventual physical death. Why? Because Yahweh breaks from what is normative in ancient Near Eastern religion in favor of showing grace and mercy. If you're familiar with the work of Jesus Christ, you know this is far from the last time God is merciful and gracious to humanity.

One of my favorite quotations of all time is from a Franciscan monk named Richard Rohr, and it applies beautifully here: "Every time God forgives, God is saying that relationship is more important than God's own rules."[16]

Adam and Eve's disobedience elicits the first demonstration of God's character. The second comes in Genesis 3, right after God enumerates the natural consequences of their sin: "The LORD God made garments of skin for Adam and his wife and clothed them" (3:21). Adam and Eve are ashamed and aware of their nakedness for the first time, so God gives them clothes to wear. Even if that were the whole story, it provides a beautiful example of God being unnecessarily kind. God doesn't have to clothe them; he could have easily left them in their fig leaves, exposed to harsh weather and other elements of nature.

Instead, God notices how ashamed they feel, and even after they have turned their backs on him, God displays affection for them. But it's even more than that, because removing someone's clothes signified removing their inheritance in many ancient cultures, stripping them down literally meant stripping them down symbolically as well. By clothing them here, God is

16. Richard Rohr, *Falling Upward: A Spirituality for the Two Halves of Life* (Jossey-Bass, 2011), 132.

reinstating Adam and Eve as his children, declaring that they still share in his inheritance.[17]

In the book *The Drama of Scripture*, Craig Bartholomew and Michael Goheen say, "In the Old Testament, to remove someone's clothes could signify their disinheritance; God's provision of clothes for Adam and Eve is a sign to them that he has not given up on his purpose for them. They are still to bear his image in this world. They are still to 'inherit the earth.'"[18]

God spares their lives and reinstates their status as his children. That's amazing in and of itself, but there is still one more piece of God's character to be revealed, and I think it provides the most beautiful picture of God in this whole story. It's found in Genesis 3 where God addresses evil embodied in the serpent: "So the LORD God said to the serpent, 'Because you have done this, cursed are you above all livestock and all wild animals! You will crawl on your belly and you will eat dust all the days of your life. And I will put enmity between you and the woman, and between your offspring and hers; he will crush your head, and you will strike his heel'" (3:14–15).

God not only addresses humanity's needs in the moment but also promises to fix the consequences of humanity's decision to give in to the influence of evil. All the sin and sinful effects caused by Adam and Eve turning their backs on God will be remedied by God himself. Christians interpret this as the first of many messianic promises—a prediction of the coming of the "Messiah," which is based on a Hebrew word that means "Savior."

17. We see this same grace on display in the story of the prodigal son in Luke 15, specifically in verses 22–24: "But the father said to his servants, 'Quick! Bring the best robe and put it on him. Put a ring on his finger and sandals on his feet. Bring the fattened calf and kill it. Let's have a feast and celebrate. For this son of mine was dead and is alive again; he was lost and is found.' So they began to celebrate."

18. Craig G. Bartholomew and Michael W. Goheen, *The Drama of Scripture: Finding Our Place in the Biblical Story*, 3rd ed. (Baker Academic, 2024), 19.

In this passage, God is promising Jesus, a God who will stoop down and put on flesh to walk with us, just like he walked with Adam and Eve. He's promising that Jesus will crush the forces of evil that humanity succumbed to in Eden and that still plague us today. Here is how Paul puts it in a letter to the early church in Rome:

> When Adam sinned, sin entered the world. Adam's sin brought death, so death spread to everyone, for everyone sinned. . . . But there is a great difference between Adam's sin and God's gracious gift. For the sin of this one man, Adam, brought death to many. But even greater is God's wonderful grace and his gift of forgiveness to many through this other man, Jesus Christ. . . . Yes, Adam's one sin brings condemnation for everyone, but Christ's one act of righteousness brings a right relationship with God and new life for everyone. (Rom. 5:12, 15, 18 NLT)

The promised Savior has come and brought forgiveness, justification, and new life not just to Adam and Eve but to everyone.

The very moment humanity chose sin, God chose forgiveness. The second that humanity broke God's very good world, God started rebuilding it. Even though we constantly struggle, fall short, and mess up, God loves us so much that he has put on flesh in the person of Jesus, entered into our brokenness, and offered everyone new life.

Literalism and Opting Out of Christianity

When we take off the literalism lens, we clearly see that the truths found in Genesis 1–3 are so much bigger and better than attempts to conform this passage into a science textbook. The story of Adam and Eve helps us understand and find hope in the truth that on humanity's very worst day, God broke his own rules to forgive us. And even on our worst days, God still loves us and would do absolutely anything to demonstrate the depth of his love.

When we attempt to interpret Genesis 1–3 through a literalistic lens, not only do we miss something beautiful, but we also create something harmful. As long as we continue to make literalistic interpretations a litmus test for true Christian faith, people will continue to self-select out of Christianity.

Take my friend Diego. He and I crossed paths about seven years ago when he started dating a young woman who attended Restore regularly. Diego wasn't exactly thrilled about being at church, making it clear from the get-go. He said something to the effect of "Listen, I'm here because of her, but I'm not into this. I'm not a Christian, and I don't believe this stuff. I just need you to know that right off the bat."

"No problem, man. You're always welcome here." Then I smiled and said, "No pressure at all, but if you ever want to get coffee or a drink, I would love to hear why that's your first reaction to meeting me." Diego laughed and said he'd like that. We grabbed some coffee a few weeks later, and Diego had questions—a ton of them. He was completely hung up on scientific arguments about the age of the earth and evolution. As it turned out, he had a strong academic background in biology, so he wasn't buying into some of the literalistic interpretations of Genesis.

I tried to explain that not every Christian thinks the earth is only a few thousand years old or rejects evolution, but Diego was baffled. His whole life he'd heard that Christians believe the earth is six thousand years old, creation happened in six twenty-four-hour days, evolution is fake, Adam and Eve are the literal parents of all humans, and even that God buried dinosaur bones to test their faith. Okay, maybe not that last one, although I vividly remember being taught that at Vacation Bible School one year.

As Diego got older and dug deeper, he realized he didn't fit in that box, so instead of trying to squeeze himself in, he opted out of Christianity altogether. His logic told him, "This is what Christians believe. I don't believe it anymore, so I guess I'm not a Christian."

After more conversations with Diego, it became obvious how much he genuinely loved Jesus and wanted to follow him, but he'd been told there was no room for someone who believes in Jesus and evolution.

Diego's story is not uncommon. I've talked to hundreds of folks who have opted out of Christianity because they could no longer endorse a literalistic interpretation of Scripture. But here's the kicker: It's not their fault. It's the fault of Christian groups and traditions that have prioritized literalistic views of Scripture over following Jesus.

So many people have been deeply hurt and disillusioned by the literalism lens. Some quit the faith altogether. Others limp along, trudging through Sunday services and trying to engage with the Bible, but they have been deeply wounded.

The damage inflicted by the literalism lens is staggering. I love the Bible too much to surrender it to the people who say you have to believe that it's all literal or you can't be a Christian. And I love folks like Diego too much to stay quiet when this harmful lens is driving them away from the open arms of Jesus.

It's time to unveil inerrancy for what it really is—an attempt to equate the biblical interpretation of a few men with the very words of God. It's time to discard the harmful literalism lens before even more people walk away from Christianity because of it. As we've already seen, a story-centered reading of Genesis 1–3 is so much richer and more satisfying. Moving away from literalistic interpretations of Scripture opens us up to more life-giving perspectives in Genesis and beyond.

Diego got to find that out firsthand. After numerous conversations over lunch or beers, Diego realized he could follow Jesus and take science seriously. He decided to become a part of our church, and I got to baptize him in the lake downtown, surrounded by his friends and family. Since then, I've had a front-row seat to watch him flourish as a partner, father, and follower of Jesus. I've had the privilege of officiating at his wedding—he married the woman who first brought him to Restore—and dedicating their kids alongside our entire church family.

We can choose Jesus and reject literalistic interpretations that cause harm. In fact, if we are going to take the Bible seriously, I think we have to.

4

the apocalypse lens

"It's All Gonna Burn Anyway"

> If God's solution for evil is to kill people who are evil, God didn't need to send his Son—he could have just sent in the tanks.
>
> —Brian Zahnd, *Postcards from Babylon*

About ten years ago, a theology professor named Sam Storms was doing research for his book on eschatology called *Kingdom Come*. Eschatology is the branch of theology devoted to understanding the events surrounding the end of the world, so Storms was investigating what the average American Christian believed about the book of Revelation and the end times. A decade ago, there was no better way to figure this out than by visiting Christian bookstores.

Do you remember Christian bookstores? Lifeway, Mardel, and Family Christian were the three biggest, boasting a combined 450 locations nationwide. There are only 40 or so left today, but if you wanted to know what American Christians were reading in the early 2000s, the easiest way to find out was to peruse the shelves of a Christian bookstore.

So that's what Sam did. He went to a Mardel location and made his way to the end times section. He went row by row through the entire section and counted 117 different books about the end times, which told Sam just how interested American Christians were in the book of Revelation. But that wasn't the most amazing discovery he made. He classified all the books into categories based on their theological perspective and found that 102 of the 117 books were devoted to defending the end times theology popularized by the Left Behind series.[1]

This particular perspective is called . . . are you ready for this? . . . dispensational, pretribulational, premillennial eschatology. Wow, right? For our purposes, let's refer to it as Left Behind theology—a view of the end times rooted in a literalistic interpretation of Revelation (including burning suns, seven-headed beasts, and a woman riding a dragon) and culminating with a bloody war in which Jesus kills all the non-Christians and torches the earth with fire.

This theology has been the dominant perspective in American evangelical Christianity for the last 120 years, but virtually no one in the history of the church subscribed to this view until the mid-nineteenth century. In addition, when we look at global Christianity, we find this is still a minority viewpoint among biblical scholars and theologians.

But Left Behind theology remains incredibly popular in the United States. One way we can measure its prominence is by looking at the Left Behind media empire, which has produced the following:

- sixteen books in the original series (altogether they've sold over eighty million copies, and seven of the books

1. Sam Storms, *Kingdom Come: The Amillennial Alternative* (Mentor, 2013), 45.

have reached number one on the *New York Times*, *USA Today*, and *Publishers Weekly* bestseller lists)

- a Left Behind kids series totaling forty books
- a bunch of graphic novels
- an album featuring songs by Michael W. Smith, DC Talk, and Rebecca St. James
- three original movies, a TV series, and two movie reboots
- a trilogy of video games in which players can use the power of prayer to strengthen their troops in combat and wield modern military weaponry (players can also shoot nonbelievers instead of converting them, although that action costs players "spirit points," which can be recovered by pausing to pray)

Altogether the Left Behind media empire is worth hundreds of millions of dollars. But if no one believed the theology undergirding it until the nineteenth century, and most people outside the United States still don't believe it, why is it so popular here?

I believe it's because our society has been formed by retributive violence. We are a country that loves when the good guys win and, more important, when the bad guys get what's coming to them. We live in a country where superhero movies are always box office hits and video games centered on killing sell better than anywhere else in the world. *New York Times* writer Michelle Goldberg says in her review of the Left Behind series, "On one level, the attraction of the Left Behind books isn't that much different from that of Tom Clancy or Stephen King. The plotting is brisk and the characterizations Manichean. People disappear and things blow up."[2]

2. Michelle Goldberg, "Fundamentally Unsound," AlterNet, August 2, 2002, https://www.alternet.org/2002/08/fundamentally_unsound.

I'm not trying to make the case that Left Behind theology isn't compelling. I'm just asking if it's at all consistent with what Revelation actually says and who Jesus is.

Hell Houses and Apocalyptic Trauma

Not long ago, I received a text message from my friend Bo, who plays bass guitar at our church. It said, "Back in Kansas they used to do like a Christian 'haunted house' tour but it was just a play that you walked through. They show you characters who die and go to heaven or hell and then scare you into accepting Jesus in your heart. They did interviews afterward with some of the 'newborns' and I wept like a baby, so I was the pride of their event. They scared me so bad I cried and accepted Christ because the only alternative was dying in a fiery car wreck and going to hell."

Bo's text came with a two-minute clip from an old promotional video shot by a company called Judgement House. I clicked the play button and what I saw brought me to tears. The video opens with two young kids saying things like "Oh my God, I hope this don't happen to me" and "I hope I don't go to hell." Then it cuts to a young boy who is sobbing—it's Bo. Through tears, little Bo says, "I got really scared when I saw hell." He goes on to say he accepted Jesus into his heart that night, even though he thought he already had, because of just how terrifying his experience was.

Do you want to guess how old Bo was in that video? Eight. He was a second grader when he was traumatized by depictions of people being tortured in hell, scared into "accepting Christ," and had a camera shoved in his face while he was still crying. That footage was used to raise money so more kids could be traumatized in other towns.

Judgement House is still traveling the country, hosting these "plays." Their website boasts that more than five million people have walked through one of their hell houses in the past forty years.[3]

After I shared Bo's story one Sunday at our church, dozens of folks came up to me and said that they too had been through a hell house. Maybe you have experience with Judgement House and maybe you don't, but I know that many of you reading this right now grew up with apocalyptic theology that terrified you with visions of the world burning, family members being raptured, and all hell breaking loose. This fear-based teaching has landed many people in therapy. It's uneasily similar to some of the teachings of cults like the Branch Davidians, led by David Koresh, and the Peoples Temple, led by Jim Jones, in which hundreds of people lost their lives. This second harmful interpretive lens, the apocalypse lens, has a literal body count.

The Invention of Left Behind Theology

Even though Left Behind theology remains the most popular framework for interpreting Revelation in modern American evangelicalism, it arises from the teachings of an English Bible teacher named John Nelson Darby from the 1830s. Some people believe he stole it from a fifteen-year-old girl named Margaret MacDonald after he overheard her speaking in tongues and prophesying during a charismatic tent revival in rural Scotland.[4] That was a wild sentence, wasn't it?

Regardless of the origins, few people would have heard of it until the late 1800s, when a man named Dwight L. Moody started preaching it. It was then popularized by institutions like

3. "Judgement House: A History," Judgement House, accessed January 3, 2025, https://www.judgementhouse.org/history.

4. For more on this, see Dave MacPherson, *The Great Rapture Hoax* (New Puritan Library, 1983); and Daniel G. Hummel, *The Rise and Fall of Dispensationalism: How the Evangelical Battle Over the End Times Shaped a Nation* (Eerdmans, 2023).

Moody Bible and Dallas Theological Seminary (my alma mater), by the Scofield Reference Bible in the early twentieth century, later by preachers like Jerry Falwell and Billy Graham, and by books like Hal Lindsey's *The Late Great Planet Earth* and the Left Behind series.

The problems with Left Behind theology are myriad; here are three of the most significant issues:

1. It ignores the genre, context, author's intent, and original audience of the book of Revelation, as well as the Old Testament references within it.
2. It turns Jesus into a retributive avenger who comes back to earth to kill everyone who doesn't worship him, a depiction wholly incompatible with the Jesus we meet in the Gospel accounts.
3. It enables pastors, politicians, and other powerful people to use the Bible to demonize their enemies and justify Revelation-like violence toward them. We've seen this happen with Muslims, LGBTQ+ folks, political leaders on both the right and the left, Jews, Palestinians, Russians, Iraqis, Iranians, Syrians, and on and on.

Both churches I grew up in, as well as the seminary I graduated from, used the apocalypse lens to claim that Revelation contains a hidden code that can be used to decipher events leading up to the end of the world. It was presented like a secret message written in invisible ink on the back of the Declaration of Independence, and we are all like Nicolas Cage, doing whatever we can to solve the riddle and save the world.

But what if John of Patmos, the author of Revelation, is not attempting to describe characters and events connected to the end times? What if he is using rich and oftentimes bizarre images and metaphors to make larger points? This is something done throughout the biblical narrative and something we still do in modern times. Think of political cartoons. A drawing of elephants and donkeys wrestling in a cage isn't meant to depict a literal exhibit at your local zoo; it is a creative representation of America's major political parties' constant quarreling. I love how Jeremy Duncan puts it in his wonderful book *Upside-Down Apocalypse*: "John does not believe in literal dragons and beasts and very scary grasshoppers. He believes in the ability of art to illuminate the world."[5]

The symbols and metaphors in the book of Revelation are meant to reveal how evil is at work in the world and how we can faithfully follow Jesus by standing against it. New Testament scholar Robyn Whitaker says it perfectly in her commentary on Revelation: "By looking at what images and symbols meant in that ancient time and place, we discover that Revelation is a highly political, but also deeply theological, text. It offers us a profound way to think about evil as something found in structures and systems, and to ponder what an ethical response to such evil might be."[6]

Revelation's art and metaphors are based on both first-century culture and Jewish Scripture. In fact, Revelation contains over 350 direct quotations from or clear allusions to the Old Testament. Many modern readers have mistakenly ignored this in favor of making the metaphors about themselves—an eagle saving Israel becomes the United States of America, locusts with tails like scorpions become Apache helicopters, and so on. These poor interpretations have not only influenced American foreign policy over the last century, they have also led to extreme fear, anxiety, and spiritual abuse.

5. Jeremy Duncan, *Upside-Down Apocalypse: Grounding Revelation in the Gospel of Peace* (Herald Press, 2022), 35–36.

6. Robyn Whitaker, *Revelation for Normal People: A Guide to the Strangest and Most Dangerous Book in the Bible* (Bible for Normal People, 2023), introduction, Kindle.

A Better Way to Read Revelation

So if we shouldn't use Left Behind theology and the apocalypse lens to interpret Revelation, how should we engage with it? Is there a better way?

First, it's important to note that Revelation is a combination of two genres of literature: apocalypse and prophecy. Apocalypse as an ancient genre is not at all what we mean when we use that word today, which is basically a synonym for annihilation or Armageddon. In the culture and language of the Bible, "apocalypse" means "unveiling" or "revealing," which is how the book got its name. But again, this isn't the revealing of a secret code to help us decipher end time events or an unveiling of church history across time. It is the revelation—to the original audience—of how to follow Jesus and why they could find hope amid the anti-Christian empire all around them. Whitaker puts it succinctly: "Revelation in its context [is] a piece of Christian resistance literature written to help first-century Christ followers navigate life within the Roman Empire."[7]

Revelation is also written in the prophetic genre, which is best understood as warnings against injustice alongside promises of a hopeful future. While researching for this chapter, I came across my seminary notes from my class on Revelation, including the paper I wrote about the book in July 2011. I braced for the worst as I opened the document, but while much of my end times theology has certainly changed since then, I was encouraged to find this line in the introduction: "It is difficult to decipher the overall message of the book of Revelation because of its diversity throughout, but even considering the various genres and themes, the overall message of the book is hope."

This hope does not come from the ability to decipher secret codes or accurately predict the end of the world. This hope is

7. Whitaker, *Revelation for Normal People*, introduction.

firmly rooted in the person and work of Jesus Christ, who has conquered death and whose reign will outlast the empires of the world. And this hope culminates in the restoration of everything broken: "Look! God's dwelling place is now among the people, and he will dwell with them. They will be his people, and God himself will be with them and be their God. 'He will wipe every tear from their eyes. There will be no more death' or mourning or crying or pain, for the old order of things has passed away" (Rev. 21:3–4).

Here's Duncan again:

> John never imagined us building a complex timeline with each beast and dragon and battle mapped out in excruciating linear detail. Instead, he hoped we might sit back, immersed in the images, marveling at all the ways we see salvation come alive in Jesus. Revelation is telling us the same story from different vantage points.
>
> And each time the story repeats, we add a new perspective to our faith, a new commitment to the way of Jesus, and new confidence in the lordship of Christ. In Revelation, there is personal transformation. That is salvation. There's politics and the crumbling of empires built on violence and greed. That is also salvation. There's the disarming of evil and the cosmic triumph of life over death. And that, too, is salvation. But all this is part of one story about how Jesus saves the world. For John, none of these perspectives are at odds. Personal transformation, social justice, and cosmic healing are implications of a victory already won. The challenge is expanding our imagination wide enough to take it all in.[8]

It's not enough to simply "leave behind" an apocalypse lens. (See what I did there?) We also have to expand our imaginations to see Jesus working for humanity's freedom and flourishing

8. Duncan, *Upside-Down Apocalypse*, 48–49.

in a myriad of ways and then join him in that work. That's how Revelation was understood by the original audience and how it should be interpreted today.

Revelation was written with the primary goal of encouraging early Christians to continue following the way of Jesus while under the thumb of the oppressive Roman Empire and to help them find hope in the fact that God is at work to end all oppression.

It wasn't just persecution that these early Christians were struggling with. The way of empire was wholly incompatible with the way of Jesus. John uses this book to exhort early Christians to choose Christlikeness. Much like empires of today, Rome chose war over peace, hierarchy over equality, the enrichment of a few over taking care of everyone, and it used fear, shame, and violence to maintain power. Christians today face similar concerns as we attempt to live out our faith:

- In communities where hatred of anyone who disagrees with us is normal, how do we love our enemies?
- In a country fueled by a military industrial complex, how do we pursue peacemaking?
- In a society where violence is commonplace, how do we practice nonviolence?
- In campaigns filled with demonization and dehumanization, how do we resist political polarization and engage with grace?
- In a world where greed and materialism are exalted, how do we take seriously the biblical truth that "the love of money is a root of all kinds of evil" (1 Tim. 6:10)?
- In a culture where lording power over others is admired, how do we implement the servant leadership Jesus has prescribed?

Even though Revelation was written to the first-century church, choosing the way of Jesus over the way of empire is vitally important for the twenty-first-century church too. And even though we American Christians aren't oppressed for our faith, it's vitally important that we fight against oppression anywhere it is found. Finally, just like those early Christians, we need to be reminded that God is at work and that we can choose hope regardless of what we're walking through.

In his book *Revelation for the Rest of Us*, Scot McKnight calls those who follow Jesus in the midst of empire "dissident disciples." He says, "John wrote the Book of Revelation for dissident disciples. He wrote it for those . . . who were willing to die before they would compromise, who would resist the empire at any cost. This is a book that calls us to civil disobedience. A dissident is a person of hope, someone who imagines a better, future world, and then begins to embody that world. It's someone who speaks to promote that better, future vision and against what is wrong in the present."[9]

New Testament scholar Richard Hays similarly asserts that we should understand Revelation as a call to justice work:

> Revelation can be read rightly only by those who are actively struggling against injustice. If Revelation is a resistance document, its significance will become clear only to those who are engaged in resistance. It is no coincidence that the most powerful modern readings of Revelation have come from interpreters in socially marginalized positions who were seeking to call the church to countercultural resistance movements: for example, Martin Luther King, Jr. (pastor and civil rights leader), William Stringfellow (pastor and social justice advocate), and Alan Boesak (pastor and anti-apartheid activist). Something very strange

9. Scot McKnight, *Revelation for the Rest of Us: A Prophetic Call to Follow Jesus as a Dissident Disciple*, with Cody Matchett (Zondervan, 2023), 17.

> happens when this text is appropriated by readers in a comfortable, powerful, majority community: it becomes a gold mine for paranoid fantasies and for those who want to preach revenge and destruction.[10]

It is long past time that we abandon paranoid fantasies about the end times promoted by an apocalyptic worldview. We must stand up against Revelation being used to promote revenge, justify war, and traumatize kids like Bo. Interpretations made using the apocalypse lens not only are completely without merit, they also really hurt people.

But What About Hell?

A discussion about the apocalypse lens would not be complete without touching on hell; the threat of spending eternity weeping and gnashing our teeth in fire and brimstone is a core part of the faith many of us grew up with. In many ways, hell is the ultimate trump card. If not following the tenets and cultural norms of American evangelicalism means burning in hell forever, why would anyone ever rock the boat?

I recently had lunch with a pastor here in Austin. He reached out to me under the guise of connecting with young people in our city, but not five minutes after we ordered, he glared at me over our basket of chips and salsa and said, "If you continue down this path, young man, you are going to spend eternity in the fires of hell. Do you know what hell is like, Zach? It's horrible. Do you really want to go to hell?"

I ended up taking my enchiladas to go, for obvious reasons, but not before he condemned me to the fiery inferno a few more

10. Richard B. Hays, *The Moral Vision of the New Testament: Community, Cross, New Creation; A Contemporary Introduction to New Testament Ethics* (HarperSanFrancisco, 1996), 108.

times. That pastor's description of hell, like that of most folks who interpret the Bible through an apocalypse lens, actually has little to do with anything the biblical authors claim.

We've taken the word "hell," an Old English word originating more than seven hundred years after Jesus, and developed a picture of it based on some combination of medieval torture chambers and Dante's *Inferno*. We have then taken that understanding of hell and applied it to every usage of the word in the Bible, writing books and preaching sermons based on this flawed definition, thus disseminating an understanding of hell to the world that is massively different from what the Bible actually teaches.

Not great, right? It comes as no shock to most of us that the results of such an understanding of hell have been a disaster. A hell more informed by Dante than by Jesus not only produces completely unnecessary fear and anxiety, it also perverts our understanding of God.

Scripture teaches very clearly that God is love: "Dear friends, let us love one another, for love comes from God. Everyone who loves has been born of God and knows God. Whoever does not love does not know God, because God is love" (1 John 4:7–8). This passage doesn't say, "God loves." It says, "God *is* love." Love is God's primary characteristic; every other characteristic flows through his love. Is God just? Yes, but that justice is loving. Is God faithful? Yes, because God stops at nothing to demonstrate his love. The unbiblical understanding of hell paints a picture of a God who is instead sadistic, vindictive, and malevolent.

Is God sadistic? Does he derive pleasure from inflicting pain on his image-bearing creation? Everything I read in Scripture tells me no.

Is God vindictive? Does he destine anyone who chooses to live their life apart from him to be burned alive and eaten by worms for eternity? Every biblical demonstration of God pursuing humanity with his love tells me no.

Is God malevolent? Does he wish evil on humanity? Every story of God graciously forgiving tells me no.

It's also worth pointing out that hell is not exactly a frequently discussed concept in Scripture. Frequency of use doesn't always equal importance, but it makes sense that the more we talk about something, the more it matters to us. Spend time with someone and you'll soon realize that what they talk about most is usually what matters to them most.

The Bible is similar. Here are the most popular subjects in the Bible based on how many times the corresponding words are used:

Lord—6,749	Israel—2,431
God—3,995	Jesus—1,310

Makes sense, right? Those are four pretty big ones.

Here are a few other important topics and how many times the coinciding words are used:

earth—729	sin—441
heaven—622	evil—430
Spirit—536	judgment—366
death—465	

By comparison, the number of times "hell" is mentioned in the Bible is 13. All in all, more than 1,200 words in the Bible are used more frequently than "hell." In light of the grand scheme of the biblical story, evangelical Christianity has significantly overrepresented hell in its writing and teaching, transforming it into something the Bible simply doesn't teach. You might be surprised to hear that 11 of the 13 uses of the word "hell" come from the mouth of Jesus. He talked about it more than anyone, but he didn't talk about it the way most people talk about it today.

Let me show you what I mean. Here's Jesus from the Sermon on the Mount:

> You have heard that it was said, "You shall not commit adultery." But I tell you that anyone who looks at a woman lustfully has already committed adultery with her in his heart. If your right eye causes you to stumble, gouge it out and throw it away. It is better for you to lose one part of your body than for your whole body to be thrown into hell. And if your right hand causes you to stumble, cut it off and throw it away. It is better for you to lose one part of your body than for your whole body to go into hell. (Matt. 5:27–30)

Jesus says it's better to cut out our eyes than to look lustfully at someone, stating that if we do look lustfully, we will be thrown into hell. Surely Jesus isn't promising eternity in an underground torture chamber for those who've lusted but haven't gouged out their eyes. So what is he really saying here? To answer that question, we must understand that every time he speaks of hell, Jesus uses the Greek word "Gehenna." The word translates to "Valley of Ben Hinnom," and it is a real location south of Jerusalem where children were sacrificed with fire in the eighth century BC. The Old Testament book of 2 Chronicles records this: "Ahaz was twenty years old when he became king, and he reigned in Jerusalem sixteen years. Unlike David his father, he did not do what was right in the eyes of the Lord. He followed the ways of the kings of Israel and also made idols for worshiping the Baals. He burned sacrifices in the Valley of Ben Hinnom and sacrificed his children in the fire, engaging in the detestable practices of the nations the Lord had driven out before the Israelites" (2 Chron. 28:1–3).

In the time of Jesus, mentioning the name Gehenna evoked images of fire, evil, and pain.[11] All this helps us to understand, like the original audience did, that Jesus and everyone else in the Bible used metaphor and imagery to describe hell.

Its Gates Will Never Be Shut

The biblical authors are not univocal in their descriptions of hell; however, there is a compelling picture of what happens to those "in hell" when Jesus returns to complete his mission of making all things new in something called the new heaven and new earth. Listen to John's description: "I did not see a temple in the city, because the Lord God Almighty and the Lamb are its temple. The city does not need the sun or the moon to shine on it, for the glory of God gives it light, and the Lamb is its lamp. The nations will walk by its light, and the kings of the earth will bring their splendor into it. On no day will its gates ever be shut" (Rev. 21:22–25). John declares that the city doesn't have a temple—the place where people went to seek forgiveness and commune with God. Why? Because everyone has already been forgiven and God walks among the people in this new heaven and new earth. There is no need for a temple because now the whole place is a temple of the Lord!

John also announces that this city's gates will never be shut. They are forever open to anyone who wants to come in. This is important, because John describes people who are outside the city: "Nothing impure will ever enter it, nor will anyone who does what is shameful or deceitful. . . . Outside are the dogs, those who practice magic arts, the sexually immoral, the

11. Amy-Jill Levine and Marc Zvi Brettler, eds., *The Jewish Annotated New Testament* (Oxford University Press, 2011), 790.

murderers, the idolaters and everyone who loves and practices falsehood" (Rev. 21:27; 22:15). Why are all these people outside the city? Because the new heaven and new earth is a place where there is no more death or pain or oppression; those outside have refused to leave behind practices that hurt themselves and others. They are seemingly in a kind of "hell."

But that's not the end of the story. Listen to what John says right after he lists the people choosing harmful practices: "The Spirit and the bride say, 'Come.' Let anyone who hears this say, 'Come.' Let anyone who is thirsty come. Let anyone who desires drink freely from the water of life" (Rev. 22:17 NLT). The picture John paints for us in these final two chapters of the Bible is of a restored world defined by fullness, flourishing, and God dwelling with humanity in a beautiful city. Outside this city are those who have yet to accept the life-changing love of Jesus and leave behind their harmful ways, but there is an eternal invitation for them to do just that—to put down the things that are hurting them and their neighbors and come into the new heaven and new earth.

Bradley Jersak puts it like this in his book *Her Gates Will Never Be Shut*: "The simple math of the New Jerusalem Gospel is beautiful and powerful, even surprising: The wicked are outside the city + the gates of the city will never be shut + the Spirit and the Bride say, 'Come!'"[12] Just like the dad waiting on his prodigal son, God patiently waits for all his children to come home. The gates are always open, and God's Spirit is forever calling, "'Come.' Let anyone who is thirsty come. Let anyone who desires drink freely from the water of life" (Rev. 22:17 NLT).

While Christians of sincere faith come to different conclusions about the final judgment—especially given the multivalent images throughout Scripture—I believe all people will

12. Bradley Jersak, *Her Gates Will Never Be Shut: Hope, Hell, and the New Jerusalem* (Wipf & Stock, 2005), 171.

eventually choose to enter those forever-open gates and experience full flourishing with God and the rest of humanity.

Here's the thing about God: From Genesis to Revelation, God never gives up on us. God keeps pursuing us with relentless love. No matter how long it takes, God will be there waiting with arms open, ready to welcome all people into the new heaven and new earth. This view is commonly called universal reconciliation through Christ. And this is not a radically new idea; consider that Clement and Origen of Alexandria, Gregory of Nyssa, C. S. Lewis, George MacDonald, Karl Barth, and four of the six early church catechetical schools all believed some version of the notion that all creation will be saved. Also consider a few other verses from Scripture:

> Just as one trespass resulted in condemnation for all people, so also one righteous act resulted in justification and life for all people. (Rom. 5:18)

> For as in Adam all die, so in Christ all will be made alive. (1 Cor. 15:22)

> For Christ's love compels us, because we are convinced that one died for all. (2 Cor. 5:14)

> I, when I am lifted up from the earth, will draw all people to myself. (Jesus in John 12:32)

When I tell people that's what I believe, a common rebuttal is something like "Then why tell anyone about Jesus now if everyone is going to be saved someday?"

My response is simple: I want everyone to be set free from the things harming them and experience flourishing through Christ as soon as possible! Like Jesus says in the Lord's Prayer, I want God's kingdom to come on earth as it is in heaven.

Most Christians think the biblical narrative culminates with some people going to heaven and others going to hell. Instead, Scripture teaches not that we will go up to heaven to meet God but that God keeps coming down out of heaven to meet us. We see it in the garden of Eden when God comes down to walk and talk with Adam and Eve. We see it when God comes down and wrestles with Jacob and when God comes down to meet with Moses on Mount Sinai. We see God come down as a burning bush, a cloud, a pillar of fire, a dove, and even a human being in the person of Jesus Christ—the ultimate "God come down" moment. John describes this in his account of Jesus's life as God becoming flesh and making his home with us (see John 1:14). And we see it when God comes down in Spirit on Pentecost when the church is born in Acts 2.

Finally, we see God come down in fullness forever in Revelation 21:

> Then I saw "a new heaven and a new earth," for the first heaven and the first earth had passed away, and there was no longer any sea. I saw the Holy City, the new Jerusalem, coming down out of heaven from God, prepared as a bride beautifully dressed for her husband. And I heard a loud voice from the throne saying, "Look! God's dwelling place is now among the people, and he will dwell with them. They will be his people, and God himself will be with them and be their God. 'He will wipe every tear from their eyes. There will be no more death' or mourning or crying or pain, for the old order of things has passed away." He who was seated on the throne said, "I am making everything new!" Then he said, "Write this down, for these words are trustworthy and true." (21:1–5)

Scripture rebuts the "it's all gonna burn anyway" theology that undergirds the nihilistic posture so many Christians have toward the earth and everything in it. God is not destroying this world; he is restoring it. God isn't abandoning creation; he is making it new! If we take off the apocalypse lens, we have a much more compelling story to tell than Left Behind fan fiction.

5

the moralism lens

"Well, That's Not Biblical"

> When we were told to "love everybody" I had thought that meant everybody. But no. It applied to only those who believed as we did.
>
> —James Baldwin, *The Fire Next Time*

I first met Brianna after she filled out one of our connect cards at church. Her card stuck out to me because in the section on the back where a person can write prayer requests, she had scribbled, "I have questions. A lot of questions."

These are my favorite kinds of cards to get, so the next day I reached out to her and asked if she wanted to meet up. She texted me back almost immediately: "How about coffee this afternoon?" A few hours later, we were sitting in the back corner of a coffee shop patio. It was one of those blisteringly hot June days in Austin, but Brianna insisted that we sit outside, far from other customers.

Before either of us even spoke, she had tears in her eyes. In a broken voice, she asked me if the Bible says God hates divorce. I replied, "The teaching regarding divorce from Scripture is much more complicated than a three-word phrase. Did someone tell you that or did you read it somewhere?"

The tears really started to fall now as Brianna said that her pastor did. Between sobs, Brianna told me about her violent ex-husband and the years she spent suffering in an abusive marriage because she was convinced that God hates divorce.

Brianna's voice rose as she recounted one of the many meetings she had with her pastor. "I came in with bruises on my arms, and he literally said, 'I know it's painful now, but it's nothing compared to the pain of God's wrath that comes with divorce. The Bible is a rule book that tells us right from wrong. If we break the rules and choose what we know is wrong, there are severe consequences. And the Bible is clear: God hates divorce.'"

At this point she was full-on weeping, and I couldn't hold back my own tears. I was devastated for Brianna and disgusted with her ex-husband, but more than anything else, I was furious with her pastor.

It's important to acknowledge that this pastor's view about divorce is not uncommon. In fact, the pastor she referred to leads a church that's seen by many as progressive. This teaching about divorce crosses the theological and ideological spectrums. When asked about divorce and abuse, pastor and author John Piper once infamously said, "If it's not requiring her to sin, but simply hurting her, then I think she endures verbal abuse for a season, and she endures perhaps being smacked one night."[1]

1. "John Piper: Does a Women [*sic*] Submit to Abuse?," posted September 1, 2009, by eaandfaith, YouTube, 3 min., 57 sec., https://youtu.be/3OkUPc2NLrM.

The most common refrain about divorce in the churches where I grew up was "You can kill him, but you can't divorce him." It was tongue in cheek, but there was no doubt that divorce simply wasn't an option for most people if they wanted to be accepted in these Christian communities.

I graduated from a Christian college and an evangelical seminary. I've worked in churches since I was nineteen years old. Pastors and pastors-in-training in those spaces are consistently taught that the singular goal in marriage counseling is to keep the couple together because "God hates divorce."

This is what happens when we read the Bible through a moralism lens: Scripture becomes a rigid rule book that exists to teach us right from wrong. I understand why this lens is attractive. Read through the lens of moralism, the Bible tells us exactly what we're supposed to do and not do. There is no ambiguity. In a society shaped by law-and-order principles, reading the Bible as the ultimate rule book is alluring.

And let's be honest, sometimes this lens works. The sixth commandment is a great example. Exodus 20:13 says, "You shall not murder." Both Christians and Jews have long considered this verse a moralistic imperative presented in no uncertain terms. Murder is wrong.

But what happens when we try to apply this lens of moralism more widely? The verse immediately preceding Exodus 20:13 is the fifth commandment, "Honor your father and your mother." And yet in the Gospel of Luke, Jesus says, "If anyone comes to me and does not hate father and mother, wife and children, brothers and sisters—yes, even their own life—such a person cannot be my disciple" (Luke 14:26). What do we do in this situation? How can we make a moral judgment regarding such blatantly conflicting verses? We can't. At least, we can't if we are committed to interpreting the Bible through the lens of moralism.

In Luke 14, Jesus is talking about the possible costs of following him. Right after he makes the statement about hating one's family, he says, "And whoever does not carry their cross and follow me cannot be my disciple. Suppose one of you wants to build a tower. Won't you first sit down and estimate the cost to see if you have enough money to complete it? For if you lay the foundation and are not able to finish it, everyone who sees it will ridicule you, saying, 'This person began to build and wasn't able to finish'" (14:27–30).

Jesus knows that he will eventually be executed by the Roman Empire for his radical way of loving God and his neighbor. He also knows that many of his followers will meet the same fate. Jesus is not making a moral statement when he talks about hating one's family. He is using hyperbole to emphasize the truth that following him will come with great consequences and that anyone who desires to do so must count the cost first.

This is why understanding the lenses through which we read Scripture is so vitally important. When we realize that Jesus is not teaching a moral imperative, we can remove that lens and interpret his words more accurately.

Divorce and Patriarchy

So what about the passage in Malachi that depicts God as saying, "I hate divorce" (see Mal. 2:16)? It seems black and white. The application of interpreting this passage through the moralism lens is straightforward: Marriage is right; divorce is wrong. But what happens when the marriage itself isn't right? What happens when a marriage is filled with abuse, neglect, pain, and suffering? Does God permit divorce in those circumstances?

To better answer these questions, we have to examine the broader teachings of Scripture regarding divorce. When we do that, the first thing we notice is that virtually every command related to divorce in the Bible is directed toward men. For instance, consider the following examples from the Old Testament:

> He writes her a certificate of divorce . . . (Deut. 24:1)

> . . . sent her away with a decree of divorce. (Jer. 3:8 ESV)

> The man who hates and divorces his wife . . . (Mal. 2:16)

Now look at these passages from the New Testament:

> Anyone who divorces his wife . . . (Matt. 5:31)

> Is it lawful for a man to divorce his wife for any and every cause? (Matt. 19:3)

> Anyone who divorces his wife . . . (Luke 16:18)

> A husband must not divorce his wife. (1 Cor. 7:11)

Why are all these passages directed toward men? Because in the Old and New Testament worlds, men wielded all the power. In Jesus's own time, women couldn't legally do much of anything, including seek a divorce. This culture was a totalitarian patriarchy, which is basically a fancy way of saying that wealthy, free men ruled everything.

This environment had two disturbing implications for women when it came to marriage and divorce. First, women had no voice in whom they would marry. A woman's father chose her husband, and the two would negotiate the terms of the marriage, most of which were financial. This was usually done when she was thirteen or fourteen years old, but sometimes she was as young as age seven. Second, women couldn't divorce their husbands for any reason. Only a man could initiate divorce. Women also had no legal rights or recourse.

Women were treated as possessions and existed to benefit the men who owned them. In first-century society, where women were essentially property, divorce was often a death sentence for a woman. Divorced women were considered damaged goods, and many resorted to begging or prostitution just to eat.

So, yes, the Bible does say that God hates divorce, but that's because God hates everything that oppresses and marginalizes people—which is exactly what happened to most divorced women in the ancient world. In a tragic twist of irony, pastors often use the expression "God hates divorce" to *keep* women in abusive marriages (inclusive of abandonment and adultery, as well as physical, sexual, verbal, psychological, financial, and spiritual abuse), which causes them to keep experiencing the very oppression God hates.

When we use passages about divorce this way, we end up doing the exact opposite of what God desires. The Bible says "God hates divorce" because divorce marginalized women in biblical cultures. But do you know what God hates way more than divorce? Weaponizing Scripture in ways that hurt people—and that's exactly what we do when we use the phrase "God hates divorce" to keep people in abusive marriages.

"Go and Sin No More"

The response I often get when I advocate for removing the moralism lens from our Bible reading is something like "So morality doesn't matter and people should just do whatever they want? What about sin? Jesus said, 'Go and sin no more.' Should we just ignore that?"

I hear some version of this argument frequently on social media. I think this is one of the most frequently misused quotations from Jesus in all of Scripture. Here are some examples I've heard recently:

> "Jesus wasn't inclusive toward sinners. He said, 'Go and sin no more.'"
>
> "No one is accepted by God until they follow his command to 'go and sin no more.'"
>
> "Stop telling people Jesus loves them unconditionally. He didn't tell them that. He told them to 'go and sin no more.'"

What did Jesus mean by this exhortation? And how does it intersect with the moralism lens? This phrase comes from a story in John's account of Jesus's life:

> Jesus returned to the Mount of Olives, but early the next morning he was back again at the Temple. A crowd soon gathered, and he sat down and taught them. As he was speaking, the teachers of religious law and the Pharisees brought a woman who had been caught in the act of adultery. They put her in front of the crowd.
>
> "Teacher," they said to Jesus, "this woman was caught in the act of adultery. The law of Moses says to stone her. What do you say?" They were trying to trap him into saying something they could use against him. (John 8:1–6 NLT)[2]

There is no question about why this woman is brought before Jesus. John says it directly: a group of scribes and Pharisees are trying to trick Jesus into saying something that will discredit him in the eyes of the crowds following him.

Now Jesus is a religious teacher in his own right, a colleague of sorts with the leaders who fling this woman down in front of him. The accounts of Jesus's life record numerous disagreements between them, many of which center on how to interpret the

2. Here and throughout this chapter, the NLT is used for quotations from John 8.

Jewish Scriptures. Jesus has a penchant for reading the Scriptures outside a moralistic framework; he consistently chooses to interpret them in ways that are more concerned with God's heart for all people to flourish than the letter of the law.

This tendency made Jesus quite disruptive to the power structures of his time. Although he frequently taught in the temple and synagogues, he also took his message to the people—beyond the boundaries and hierarchies of his religious context. Jesus continually proclaimed the truth that all people are loved by God, not because of who they are or what they have done but because they are God's children, and there isn't anything they can do to make him love them any more or less. Although Jesus was committed to the law of Moses, he subordinated everything to this message of God's unconditional love and radical acceptance.

We see the moralism lens at work in John 8 when the men bring the woman caught in adultery to Jesus. To them, the biblical text is black and white. This woman sinned, her sin is punishable by death according to the law of Moses, and therefore she should be executed. That's why they phrase the question this way: "Teacher, . . . this woman was caught in the act of adultery. The law of Moses says to stone her. What do you say?" (8:4–5).

For reference, here is what the law of Moses says on this subject: "If a man commits adultery with another man's wife—with the wife of his neighbor—both the adulterer and the adulteress are to be put to death" (Lev. 20:10). Why was only the woman (the "adulteress") brought before Jesus? Where is the adulterer? The law of Moses also required two eyewitnesses (Deut. 19:15). Where are they? Even the judicial proceedings prescribed by the law are ignored. The woman's accusers are selectively quoting and selectively applying the law of Moses—something that often happens when we interpret the Bible through a moralistic lens.

Jesus seemingly must choose between breaking the law of Moses or being a party to the killing of this woman. If he chooses the former, her accusers will say, "We told you he wasn't really from God. He doesn't even obey God's laws!" If he chooses the latter, he will undermine his message of God's unconditional love and radical acceptance. Let's see what happens: "Jesus stooped down and wrote in the dust with his finger" (John 8:6).

No one knows what he wrote. Some think he was writing the names of the other adulterers present; others think he was listing the sins of the men holding stones. All we know is that he doesn't answer their question at first. Instead, he changes his posture. He goes from standing to stooping.

I imagine the woman's accusers are a little bewildered by this response, but they press forward. "They kept demanding an answer, so he stood up again and said, 'All right, but let the one who has never sinned throw the first stone!' Then he stooped down again and wrote in the dust. When the accusers heard this, they slipped away one by one, beginning with the oldest, until only Jesus was left in the middle of the crowd with the woman" (John 8:7–9).

Jesus stands up to respond to them, then returns to kneeling next to her. Jesus's posture here is vitally important. I imagine this woman is terrified—down on the ground, shaking in fear, with tears running down her cheeks. Jesus does not stand over her and argue about her right to exist. She is not a debate topic; she is a person—an image bearer of God. So Jesus stoops down to be with the woman in her pain and fear. His posture is one of care, one of advocacy, one of love.

These men would have already had stones with them when they brought the woman to Jesus, ready to throw them at her as soon as Jesus gave the word. But Jesus says, "Let the one who has never sinned throw the first stone!" (John 8:7). And they all walk away.

This is one of the most powerful scenes in all of Scripture: the accusers towering over the woman, holding stones in their hands as Jesus kneels next to her, advocating for her freedom.

Then, as the men drop their stones and walk away, Jesus turns to her and says:

> "Where are your accusers? Didn't even one of them condemn you?"
>
> "No, Lord," she said.
>
> And Jesus said, "Neither do I. Go and sin no more." (John 8:10–11)

This is the crux of the story. But it's so often twisted in order to make a point about God's judgment of sin and the moralistic nature of Scripture.

I can't tell you how many times I've heard things like "He may have kept them from killing her, but Jesus didn't just freely forgive her sin. She had to 'go and sin no more' in order to be absolved."

What? Did you even read the story? Freely forgiving and absolving her sin is exactly what Jesus does. And he defies the plain reading of the law of Moses in order to do it! I'm not making some outlandish theological claim here. This is what the passage says. According to the law, the woman deserves death for adultery. The moral code is clear. Yet Jesus prevents her death, sends her accusers away, then freely removes all judgment from her. Not because she deserves it but because he desires it.

The statement "Go and sin no more" isn't a judgment, and it's obviously not meant as a threat of condemnation. Jesus just finished saying, "I do not condemn you." Despite notions to the contrary, the condemnation of humanity is explicitly not what Jesus put on flesh and came to earth to achieve. The most famous passage in all the Bible tells us so: "For God so loved the world that he gave his one and only Son, that whoever believes in him shall not perish but have eternal life. For God did not send his Son into the world to condemn the world, but to save the world through him" (John 3:16–17). God didn't send Jesus into the world to condemn it, and God didn't send any of us into the world to condemn it either.

What has God always been about? Restoring relationship with humanity through unconditional love and radical acceptance. That's exactly what Jesus is embodying in John 8. Yes, he tells the woman to "go and sin no more," but that comes after he stoops down to offer his unconditional love and radical acceptance to her. When we break free from the moralism lens, something like "go and sin no more" becomes a manifestation of Jesus's love and his desire for our flourishing rather than a cruel condemnation.

This is a story about moralism run amok and Jesus's act of protecting the person trapped in the middle of it. When I read about this woman caught in adultery, I can't help but think of my friend Brianna. Like the woman in Scripture, she was forced into dangerous positions by men interpreting Scripture through a moralistic lens. That's why we have to be clear: The Bible is not a rigid rule book, and God is not a condemning Creator. Jesus demonstrates these two truths to us over and over again.

Moralism and Sin

Let me be clear: Morality does matter, and people shouldn't just do whatever they want. Jesus desperately wanted this woman caught in adultery to leave behind the things that were hurting her, not *so that* he could love her but *because* he already loved her. Jesus didn't love sinners and embrace outcasts to make them acceptable to God. He did it to show them, and everyone else, that God had already accepted them. By leading with acceptance, Jesus invites everyone to the table, where they can have their needs met and experience the love that transforms. Then and only then does the injunction to "go and sin no more" make sense.

I firmly believe that God wants us to leave sin behind, but not because he is some malicious legalist holding every human to an impossible moral standard or because he flies off the handle in anger anytime we do something wrong. God hates sin because sin hurts us. And God hates to see us get hurt. I love the way Jonathan Merritt says it: "God hates sin. Not because God is an angry rule-maker. But because God loves us without constraint. God wants each of us to live the abundant life. God wants peace for us. God wants shalom for us. God wants us to flourish. He wants us to recognize the divine imprint in others and support their flourishing. Any force that resists the abundant life is called 'sin,' and this is a force to which God stands opposed."[3]

Whether it's chosen by us or inflicted on us, sin prevents flourishing. And God wants absolutely everyone to experience flourishing. How do we do that? By receiving God's radical acceptance and allowing his unconditional love to transform us.

We see Jesus model this truth throughout his life. Remember Zacchaeus? He was the tax collector who enriched himself by partnering with the oppressive Roman Empire to extort his fellow citizens. When Jesus met him, he offered Zacchaeus radical acceptance and unconditional love by eating dinner with him and spending the night in his home.

Jesus never yells at Zacchaeus, never tells him to repent, doesn't say, "Stop stealing from people, or I won't have dinner with you." And how does Zacchaeus respond to the acceptance and love of Jesus? He stands up and says to the Lord, "Look, Lord! Here and now I give half of my possessions to the poor,

3. Jonathan Merritt, *Learning to Speak God from Scratch: Why Sacred Words Are Vanishing—and How We Can Revive Them* (Convergent, 2018), 129.

and if I have cheated anybody out of anything, I will pay back four times the amount" (Luke 19:8).

The love of Jesus transforms Zacchaeus, and he leaves his sinful practices behind. But love and acceptance always come first. Paul puts it bluntly in his letter to the church in Rome:

> You see, at just the right time, when we were still powerless, Christ died for the ungodly. Very rarely will anyone die for a righteous person, though for a good person someone might possibly dare to die. But God demonstrates his own love for us in this: While we were still sinners, Christ died for us. . . . Not only is this so, but we also boast in God through our Lord Jesus Christ, through whom we have now received reconciliation. (Rom. 5:6–8, 11)

Jesus came for us before we ever turned to him.

Jesus loved us before we ever loved him.

And even though we rejected God, God reconciled with us through Christ.

When people are standing over us, holding rocks in their hands, ready to belittle and bruise us, Jesus kneels next to us. This is Jesus's posture in the story of the woman caught in adultery, and it is God's posture toward all of us.

Two different times, John tells us that Jesus knelt down next to the woman: "They were trying to trap him into saying something they could use against him, but Jesus stooped down and wrote in the dust with his finger. They kept demanding an answer, so he stood up again and said, 'All right, but let the one who has never sinned throw the first stone!' Then he stooped down again and wrote in the dust" (John 8:6–8). This posture from Jesus is not new. This is who God has always been and who he will always be. Our God is a God who kneels down next to us. Even though it might seem undignified, even scandalous, God consistently chooses to move toward us. The late Rachel Held Evans says it like this: "Dignified or not, believable or not, ours is a God perpetually on bended knee, doing everything it takes to convince stubborn and petulant children that they are seen and loved."[4]

From the woman caught in adultery, to Zacchaeus, to Brianna, to you and me, our God is perpetually on bended knee, doing everything he can to help us see that we are accepted and loved.

There was only one person in the crowd that day who was without sin. Jesus was the only one who could cast the first stone, the only one who could rightfully condemn the woman. But he didn't. He accepted her instead. And he didn't tell her to get herself cleaned up first. He accepted her just as she was—lying there in the dirt, overwhelmed by guilt and shame and fear. Jesus didn't accept some future idealized version of her either. He didn't say, "Go and sin no more and then come back, and I'll make a decision about whether you get to be a part of my family or not."

No. Jesus accepted her just as she was. He loved her so much that no amount of sin or struggle could keep him from her. The same is true for you. No matter who you are or what you've done, there is only one person who has the right to condemn you—and he has chosen not to. He has chosen to accept you, to forgive you, and to love you without hesitation or qualification. Even and especially at our lowest points, God kneels down, wipes the tears from our eyes, and says, "My child, there is no condemnation with me. I love you. I always have. And I will always be by your side."

Morality matters, but reducing the Bible to a moral guide and God to a moral judge is terribly misguided. Scripture is so much

4. Rachel Held Evans, *Inspired: Slaying Giants, Walking on Water, and Loving the Bible Again* (Thomas Nelson, 2018), 12.

more than a rule book, and reading everything in it through the moralism lens not only turns the Bible into something it was never supposed to be; it also really harms people. It's time to take off the moralism lens so that we can see both Scripture and the God it describes for what they truly are.

6

the hierarchy lens

"Submit to Authority as You Submit to God"

> Empires create their own theologies to justify their occupation. . . . This is why biblical interpretation is critical. The one who interprets assumes power.
>
> —Mitri Raheb, *Faith in the Face of Empire*

Over the years, I have mellowed regarding many of the theological perspectives I used to argue with people about—atonement theories, eschatology, mode of baptism, and so on. I've learned enough about those subjects to know that smart, Jesus-loving people can disagree without conflict. But there is one issue I'm still willing to go to the mattresses[1] for: Christmas music.

Simply put, Christmas music is too good to be restricted to the holiday season. I listen to Christmas music year-round and firmly believe your life would dramatically improve if you did

1. This is both a *Godfather* and a *You've Got Mail* reference. You're welcome.

the same. My favorite Christmas song is "O Holy Night." I've loved it since I was a little kid, but I didn't know the story behind it until a few years ago, and now I love it all the more.

The story begins in the 1840s in a small town in southern France. The Catholic church in the town of Roquemaure was having its organ repaired, a process that took a few years to complete. As the repair dragged on, the parish priest decided that the church needed a special way to premiere the renovated organ when it was done.

The repairs were set to be completed around Christmastime, so the priest asked a local poet named Placide Cappeau and a local composer named Adolphe Charles Adam to work together on a new Christmas song. The goal was to debut the song at midnight Mass on Christmas in 1847, with the famous opera singer Emily Laurey singing the lyrics, accompanied by the church's newly revitalized organ.

The plan was executed flawlessly, and the song, originally called "Cantique de Noel," was a hit! It wasn't long before the catchy tune escaped the confines of that parish in Roquemaure and began to spread all over France. Its popularity quickly became an issue with the Catholic Church, however, when leaders found out that neither of the men who wrote the song was Catholic or even a churchgoer. In 1864, a Catholic journal published an article about it: "It might be a good thing to discard this piece whose popularity is becoming unhealthy. It is sung in the streets, social gatherings, and at bars with live entertainment. It becomes debased and degenerated. The best would be to let it go its own way, far from houses of religion, which can do very well without it."[2] But despite the church's best effort to

2. Cited in Benjamin Ivry, "A Brief History of 'O Holy Night,' the Rousing Christmas Hymn That Garnered Mixed Reviews," *America Magazine*, November 19, 2020, https://www.americamagazine.org/arts-culture/2020/11/19/brief-history-o-holy-night-christmas-hymn-review.

bury the song, the French continued to embrace it. And about a decade later, the song made its way across the pond to the United States of America.

John Sullivan Dwight, a Harvard College and Divinity School graduate, started his career as a pastor in Boston, but every time he stood up in front of his congregation to preach, he had a panic attack. Things got so bad that he eventually locked himself in the parsonage because he was afraid to go out in public.

At the encouragement of people who loved him, Dwight decided pastoring was probably not the vocation for him and returned to his first love—music. He founded *Dwight's Journal of Music* and spent the next three decades reviewing and publishing songs from all over the world. In 1855, he came across "Cantique de Noel" in French. He was so moved by it that he decided to translate it into English, and "O Holy Night" as we know it today was born. Dwight adored the entire song, but he especially loved verse 3:

> Truly He taught us to love one another;
> His law is love and His gospel is peace.
> Chains shall He break, for the slave is our brother,
> And in His name all oppression shall cease.

Do you know what was happening in the United States the year Dwight discovered this song? The "united" states were on the brink of civil war. At that time, America was divided into slave states, where enslaving people was legal, and free states, where enslaving people was illegal. Over the next six years, eleven Southern states would secede from the United States in an attempt to maintain the institution of chattel slavery,[3] thus bringing about the start of the Civil War.

3. Many states proclaimed slavery to be the central reason for secession. For example, South Carolina's declaration cited "an increasing hostility on the part of

Dwight, meanwhile, was a staunch abolitionist. At a time when over half of the published arguments in favor of slavery were being written by Christian pastors,[4] the ex-clergyman was publishing what would become an abolitionist anthem.

In 1855, he published "O Holy Night" in *Dwight's Journal of Music*, and the song took off, gaining immense popularity in the North during the Civil War. As you can imagine, not everyone loved it, including many religious leaders. In fact, the largest Protestant denomination in the world, the Southern Baptist Convention, had been founded in 1845 to allow clergy and missionaries to continue enslaving Black people.

Even after the Civil War was over and "O Holy Night" became one of the most well-known Christmas songs around the world, many churches in the South refused to sing verse 3 or banned the song entirely. These pastors and parishioners attended church services that were very similar to ours today. With the exception of "O Holy Night," they sang many of the same songs we still sing. But when they walked out of church after the Sunday service was over, they still treated Black people as subhuman.[5]

---

the non-slaveholding states to the institution of slavery" as their reason for seceding from the Union. State of South Carolina, South Carolina Declaration of Secession (December 24, 1860), available at https://constitutioncenter.org/the-constitution/historic-document-library/detail/south-carolina-declaration-of-secession-1860.

4. Larry E. Tise, *Proslavery: A History of the Defense of Slavery in America, 1701–1840* (University of Georgia Press, 1987), xvii.

5. This treatment happened through de jure discrimination, such as the Jim Crow laws and redlining, as well as de facto discrimination, which was baked into the culture. Tragically, we have record of lynchings being scheduled on Sundays so people could watch Black people be executed after attending church. There are many examples of this, but a famous one is the lynching of Lation Scott in Dyersburg, Tennessee, on Sunday, December 2, 1917. Scott was tortured and murdered in front of seven to eight thousand people right after churches let out. For more about Scott's lynching, see Benjamin Brawley, *A Social History of the American Negro, Being a History of the Negro Problem in the United States, including a History and Study of the Republic of Liberia* (Macmillan, 1921).

They called themselves Christians, but they didn't follow Christ.

They knew about Jesus, but they didn't pursue the way of Jesus.

They read from the very same Bible we do, but they interpreted it through a lens of hierarchy.

Those who use the hierarchy lens claim the Bible exists to tell us humanity's pecking order—who is most important, who is least important, and who lives somewhere in between. This lens is responsible for the Bible being used to justify many of the worst horrors of human history. The hierarchy lens was the lens of the Nazis. Nazi Germany was overwhelmingly a Christian nation, with the vast majority of its leaders, including Adolf Hitler, identifying as Christian. They used Christian symbols and the Scriptures to justify the ethnic cleansing of over six million Jews.

The hierarchy lens was the lens of Christians who colonized the Americas and attempted to eradicate countless indigenous communities under the guise of God's "manifest destiny." Historians estimate that ten million indigenous people were killed, while another five million were enslaved. Some of those deaths took place at the hands of Puritan Christians who used the Bible to justify an attempted genocide against the Pequot tribe in 1637. Reflecting on the attempted genocide and his role in it, Captain John Underhill wrote in his memoir, "Sometimes the Scripture declareth women and children must perish with their parents. We have sufficient light from the Word of God for our proceedings."[6]

The hierarchy lens was the lens of the Crusades, the Ku Klux Klan, the Inquisitions, and dozens of other massacres carried out in the name of God and with the justification of the Bible.

6. John Underhill, *Newes from America* (Peter Cole, 1638).

Jonathan Wilson-Hartgrove says that interpreting the Bible through the hierarchy lens leads to something called slaveholder religion. In his book *Reconstructing the Gospel: Finding Freedom from Slaveholder Religion*, Wilson-Hartgrove delves into how the Bible has been used and misused in the context of American Christianity, especially in relation to slavery and racism. He says, "Throughout history, those in power have often manipulated the interpretation of the Bible to maintain their dominance. True faith requires us to question these interpretations and seek the deeper truths of the gospel. . . . Slaveholder religion has always found ways to justify its actions with Scripture. It twists the Bible to support the status quo and sanctify the oppression of others."[7]

Biblical manipulation for the purpose of hierarchy is exemplified in the Slave Bible.[8] Originally published in 1807 and formally called "Select Parts of the Holy Bible for the Use of the Negro Slaves in the British West-India Islands," the Slave Bible edited out any parts of Scripture that referred to freedom and equality. Leaving these keys themes out meant the editors included only 10 percent of the Old Testament and about 50 percent of the New Testament. They believed "these sections, such as Exodus, the Book of Psalms, and the Book of Revelation, could instill in slaves a dangerous hope for freedom and dreams of equality."[9]

So what can be done? Should we just throw the Bible away? Frederick Douglass once said, "It is no evidence that the Bible is a bad book, because those who profess to believe the Bible are

7. Jonathan Wilson-Hartgrove, *Reconstructing the Gospel: Finding Freedom from Slaveholder Religion* (InterVarsity, 2018), 47, 77.

8. See "The Slave Bible: Let the Story Be Told," Museum of the Bible, accessed January 6, 2025, https://www.museumofthebible.org/exhibits/slave-bible.

9. Ben Zehavi, "19th-Cent. Slave Bible That Removed Exodus Story to Repress Hope Goes on Display," *Times of Israel*, March 29, 2019, https://www.timesofisrael.com/19th-cent-slave-bible-that-removed-exodus-story-to-repress-hope-goes-on-display.

bad. The slaveholders of the South, and many of their wicked allies at the North, claim the Bible for slavery; shall we, therefore, fling the Bible away as a pro-slavery book? No."[10]

I agree with Douglass. Even the editors of the Slave Bible realized that half of the New Testament and 90 percent of the Old Testament directly combat religious hierarchy and subjugation. We don't need to throw the Bible away, but we do need better ways to read it. When it comes to curing the cancer that is the hierarchy lens, there is no better antidote than liberation theology. We will talk about this theological tradition in depth in chapter 9, but one of its foundational principles is that the perspectives and interpretations of folks on society's margins hold the key to understanding core elements of Scripture and thus must be elevated for the whole church to hear. As Kat Armas writes, "While the Bible has been weaponized by oppressors, it has also served as a beacon of hope and strength by the oppressed."[11]

The First Church Fights Hierarchy

Liberation theology emerged primarily in Latin America during the late twentieth century, but the idea of lifting up marginalized people and perspectives is something the church has been doing from the beginning. The book of Acts, which records about thirty years of the early church's story, shows us what this can look like.

The church in Acts demonstrates that God is on a mission to break down hierarchies between people and create a new kind of community, one where all people stand on equal footing before God and one another. Acts tells the story of a group of

10. Frederick Douglass, *My Bondage and My Freedom* (Miller, Orton & Mulligan, 1855), 351.

11. Kat Armas, *Abuelita Faith: What Women on the Margins Teach Us About Wisdom, Persistence, and Strength* (Brazos, 2021), 13.

about one hundred people, led by Mary Magdalene, Peter, and other disciples, who had been meeting together every day since the resurrection in eager anticipation of Jesus sending the Holy Spirit to launch the church. And finally that day comes: "When the day of Pentecost came, they were all together in one place. Suddenly a sound like the blowing of a violent wind came from heaven and filled the whole house where they were sitting. They saw what seemed to be tongues of fire that separated and came to rest on each of them. All of them were filled with the Holy Spirit and began to speak in other tongues as the Spirit enabled them" (Acts 2:1–4).

These tongues are not the kind associated with charismatic churches that need interpretation. The tongues described here are various human languages. Read what happens next: "When they heard this sound, a crowd came together in bewilderment, because each one heard their own language being spoken. Utterly amazed, they asked: 'Aren't all these who are speaking Galileans? Then how is it that each of us hears them in our native language? . . . [Here the author lists eighteen countries, languages, and ethnicities.] We hear them declaring the wonders of God in our own tongues!'" (Acts 2:6–8, 11).

The first thing the Holy Spirit does is break down dividing walls of hierarchy and declare the wonders of God to all people. Ethnicity isn't a barrier, culture isn't a barrier, class isn't a barrier, even language isn't a barrier.

Now that people are gathered around this small group of Jesus followers, Peter gets up and preaches the very first sermon to the church. He starts by going back to a prophecy from the Old Testament book of Joel:

> This is what was spoken by the prophet Joel:
> "In the last days, God says,
> I will pour out my Spirit on all people.

> Your sons and daughters will prophesy,
> your young men will see visions,
> your old men will dream dreams.
> Even on my servants, both men and women,
> I will pour out my Spirit in those days." (Acts 2:16–18)

Did you catch that? The opening lines of the very first sermon to the very first church boldly declare that God intends for all people to be equally included in this new community—regardless of age or gender or class or ethnicity or anything else. I can't begin to tell you how provocative Peter's sermon would have been in first-century society, where only men of a certain age, ethnicity, and status were allowed to govern religious and cultural affairs. God is breaking down walls to create a new community of mutuality and flourishing. Some three thousand people decide to become followers of Jesus that day, and the leaders of the church baptize them right then and there.

But like with any group of people coming together from different backgrounds, it isn't long before trouble arises. Prejudices and problems they thought had previously been fixed when God had declared the old ways of hierarchy to be unacceptable start to bubble back up. Many of these issues center on the fact that Greco-Roman culture was initially dominant in the early church, largely because most of the early church leaders were from the same general region, but that quickly changes as the church attracts people from different places.

These ethnic and cultural divisions manifest into a specific problem that Luke, the author of Acts, records: "In those days when the number of disciples was increasing, the Hellenistic Jews among them complained against the Hebraic Jews because their widows were being overlooked in the daily distribution of food" (Acts 6:1).

Fault lines begin to emerge between the Hebraic Jews and the Hellenistic Jews.[12] The easiest way to think about this is majority culture versus minority culture: The majority culture has been marginalizing the minority culture based on power and social status. Commenting on this passage, author Dominique DuBois Gilliard says:

> The Hellenist widows felt as if their outsider status was causing them to be overlooked and marginalized in the church's distribution of food. The Hebraic widows had advocates at the table of power, as well as cultural, linguistic, and relational advantages that led to them receiving superior treatment. They had privilege. Meanwhile, the Hellenistic widows lacked representation at the decision-making table and were without an advocate in leadership who saw their suffering and identified with their marginalized experience. Consequently, the church did not care for Hellenistic widows with the same care, intentionality, and love as it did for Hebraic widows. The exclusively Hebraic leadership had a blind spot, and the distribution disparity went unacknowledged until Hellenistic Jews brought a formal complaint. This matter was one of the earliest challenges the church faced as it started becoming multicultural.[13]

I want you to imagine what might happen in a modern church if an issue like the one described here emerged. Many of us don't have to imagine, because we've experienced it. I've been on a church staff when one of its pastors was accused of giving one race or ethnicity preference over another, and let me tell

12. The distinction between Hebraic Jews and Hellenistic Jews was rooted in cultural and linguistic differences within the early Christian community. Hebraic Jews were native to Judea and adhered strictly to Jewish customs and traditions. They primarily spoke Hebrew or Aramaic. Hellenistic Jews were Jews of the Diaspora who had adopted the Greek language and some aspects of Greek culture. They primarily spoke Greek.

13. Dominique DuBois Gilliard, *Subversive Witness: Scripture's Call to Leverage Privilege* (Zondervan Reflective, 2021), xix.

you, it was not handled well. The leadership became defensive, they started gaslighting those who had brought the complaint by calling them crazy, and they even blame-shifted, saying it was actually the marginalized group's fault because of a defect within their culture. It was ugly.

It's easy for people with privilege to get defensive when a hierarchy problem is brought to their attention, especially if they believe their motives are good. But defensiveness is not the way of Jesus and it's never how his people should respond. Thankfully, it's not how the early church responds: "So the Twelve gathered all the disciples together and said, 'It would not be right for us to neglect the ministry of the word of God in order to wait on tables. Brothers and sisters, choose seven men from among you who are known to be full of the Spirit and wisdom. We will turn this responsibility over to them and will give our attention to prayer and the ministry of the word'" (Acts 6:2–4).

I know that the leaders saying "We shouldn't neglect the ministry of the word of God to wait on tables" sounds a little pompous, but that's why understanding context and language is so important. Serving at tables actually refers to more than giving out food. The word used here for "table" is best translated as "money table," or what modern people might call a bank account; this would be where all the church's finances were kept.

As a result, the "daily distribution" mentioned in verse 1 included more than food. Most likely, this was the distribution of the "fund" mentioned in Acts 2 and 4, the one that provided for those who didn't have enough, such as widows. Managing the daily distribution of this fund was a vitally important job and was being done in a way that marginalized the Hellenistic widows in favor of the Hebraic widows because of their ethnicity and culture.

Notice that when the church leaders hear about this problem, they don't ignore it. They don't make excuses and get defensive. They don't say things like:

> "Stop making everything about race."
>
> "Y'all are overreacting."
>
> "Yes, we're all Hebraic Jews, but this has nothing to do with ethnicity or culture."
>
> "Some of my best friends are Hellenistic Jews!"

No. They listen. They say, "This is not okay." Then they do something about it. In this case, doing something about it means appointing a group of leaders who will be tasked with making sure the Hellenistic widows don't get overlooked again. But here is the most important part—look who gets appointed: "This proposal pleased the whole group. They chose Stephen, a man full of faith and of the Holy Spirit; also Philip, Procorus, Nicanor, Timon, Parmenas, and Nicolas from Antioch, a convert to Judaism. They presented these men to the apostles, who prayed and laid their hands on them" (Acts 6:5–6).

You might not be able to tell at first glance, but this is an incredible list of leaders. Why? Because every single one of them is a Hellenist. We know from their names and from elsewhere in Scripture that each and every one of the seven men selected to solve the problem of Hellenistic widows being overlooked is a Hellenist himself. The group that has been marginalized is lifted up. These Hellenists are given positions of authority and empowered to fix the problem in the way they think is best.

It's important to point out that this solution isn't tokenization. It isn't inviting a Black choir into an all-White church for one Sunday and then pretending centuries of systemic racism are fixed. The early church addresses the problem of hierarchy not just by including the previously excluded folks but by making sure they are elevated to positions of power and leadership.

As we watch the early church progress, we see that hierarchy is an ongoing issue. Throughout Acts, people use hierarchy in an attempt to subjugate others in the name of God, but faithful church leaders courageously stand up and say no. For example:

- Some people believe those with disabilities have been cursed by God, but in Acts 3 Peter heals and welcomes those who have been disabled since birth.
- Others believe the poor deserve their plight and should remain the lowest in the caste system, but in Acts 6 Stephen gives food to the hungry and fully includes those experiencing poverty.
- Some folks think sexual minorities aren't allowed in God's new community at all, but in Acts 8 Philip witnesses to and baptizes the Ethiopian eunuch, who had previously been excluded.
- Other people believe women should be kept out of leadership roles, but in Acts 16 Paul welcomes a woman named Lydia, who goes on to start the very first Christian church in Europe inside her home.

Paul is one leader who is never afraid to address the problem of hierarchy head-on. In his letter to the Galatian church, he famously says, "So in Christ Jesus you are all children of God through faith, for all of you who were baptized into Christ have clothed yourselves with Christ. There is neither Jew nor Gentile, neither slave nor free, nor is there male and female, for you are all one in Christ Jesus" (Gal. 3:26–28).

These verses are not about uniformity; they are about unity and equality within diversity. Paul isn't saying there are no more men and women; he's saying there is no more hierarchy between men and women. He's not claiming there should be no more ethnic identities; he's saying there should be no more marginalization or segregation among ethnic groups. He's not denying distinctions between people; he's proclaiming that distinctions don't prevent Christians from living together in mutuality.

God Hates Hierarchy

We aren't meant to leave our uniqueness behind when we become followers of Jesus. In fact, a big group of diverse people coming together in equality is exactly what God has in mind for the church. We know this from the picture we have of the new heaven and new earth in Revelation: "After this I looked, and there before me was a great multitude that no one could count, from every nation, tribe, people and language, standing before the throne and before the Lamb" (7:9). Humanity in its final, glorified, and redeemed form is a humanity representative of every tribe, tongue, nation, and people group. Humanity at its best is both diverse and equal, because God hates hierarchy.

It's absolutely essential to understand that the entire Bible, especially God's work through the church in Acts, makes it clear that God is in the business of eradicating discriminatory human hierarchies in every form. All kinds of people, from all kinds of places, with all kinds of experiences standing before God and one another in equality—that is the family of God. Anything other than that, including marginalization, oppression, and interpreting the Bible through a hierarchical lens, is opposed to the mission of God.

We must find better ways to read the Bible than as a caste-system starter kit. As my friend Trey Ferguson says, "The same approach to scripture that insisted slavery & segregation were God-ordained is used to insist that the proper place for women is under men and that homosexuality is inherently sinful. All I'm askin for is consistency. If we gon stop readin like bigots, then let's stop. I seen Black men leadin integrated churches where women can't preach. I seen women preachin messages against the queer community. At some point we gotta examine the lack of integrity in our hermeneutics. We cannot read the Bible for our own liberation while caging others."[14]

We cannot read the Bible for our own liberation while caging others. Reading the Bible in ways that justify oppression and marginalization is the gospel of slaveholders. Reading the Bible in ways that lead to justice, equality, and flourishing for all is the gospel of Jesus Christ. Because "truly He taught us to love one another; His law is love and His gospel is peace. Chains shall He break, for the slave is our brother, and in His name all oppression shall cease."

14. Trey Ferguson (@PastorTrey05), "The same approach to scripture that insisted slavery & segregation were God-ordained," Twitter (now X), February 5, 2024, https://x.com/PastorTrey05/status/1754617957479587912.

part 3

lenses that promote healing

7

the jesus lens

"The Scriptures Point to Me"

> Even Scripture can be anti-Christ if we allow it to move us away from the way of Jesus.
>
> —Jeremy Duncan, *Upside-Down Apocalypse*

Christianity is not a text-centered faith. A text-centered faith is just what it sounds like: a religious tradition based on a religious text. It usually goes something like this: A god or gods hand down a set of teachings to a human or a semidivine person, that person writes everything down, and then a religion is born based on the writings or text.

In Hinduism, the Vedas were given to human sages by Brahma. In Islam, Muhammad was given the Qur'an from Allah. In Wicca, the Book of Shadows was written by Gerald Gardner under the inspiration of the Moon Goddess and

Horned God. I think we can make the case that most major world religions are text-centered faiths, with the exception of one: Christianity.

Christianity is not a text-centered faith. Christianity is a Jesus-centered faith.

Have you ever heard the notion that Christians are people of the book? That phrase actually originates with the prophet Muhammad and is first found in the Qur'an in reference to the major monotheistic religions. Monotheism is the belief in a single, preeminent deity. Muslims, Jews, and Christians all belong to a monotheistic faith and are "people of the book"—Muslims with the Qur'an, Jews with the Tanakh or Hebrew Scriptures, and Christians with the Christian Bible. But Christians are distinct in one important way: Christians are not *primarily* people of the Bible; rather, they are people of the incarnation, life, death, and resurrection of Jesus Christ. As important as the Bible is for understanding who Jesus is, our faith is not ultimately in a text but in a person. That's why we aren't called "little Bibles." We are called "little Christs." That's what "Christian" literally means: "little Christ."

This understanding of Christianity isn't novel. Professors, authors, pastors, and theologians from all different backgrounds and denominations affirm it. In fact, Christianity being Jesus-centered rather than text-centered has been the central message of Christianity for two thousand years, but we've gotten away from it lately, especially those of us who are heirs of the Protestant Reformation.

Far too often, we have elevated our preferred biblical interpretation over the work and way of Jesus Christ, and we've done so with major consequences. If we don't shift the way we speak about and live out our faith toward being centered on Jesus, we are destined to see the continued rejection of Christianity in America at even higher rates.

Deconstructing a Text-Centered Faith

In the last twenty-five years, around forty million Americans have stopped attending church.[1] Tens of millions more are deconstructing their faith. If you aren't familiar with the word "deconstruction," think of your faith as a house made of bricks. When I say "faith," I mean your beliefs, your spiritual practices, your church background, and your religious community. Each of these elements contributed bricks to your house of faith.

The building of your house most likely took place when you were young, whether you grew up in church or you were exposed to Christianity through relationships and media. Those early beliefs and practices were the first bricks laid in place and have served as the foundation for your house of faith. As you grew up, you read things, heard things, and were exposed to different people and ideas; as this occurred, you added even more bricks to your house of faith. This process is called "construction."

If you grew up in church, your house of faith was most likely constructed in a purposeful way via your parents, your pastor, your church, and possibly your denomination. Certain people have certain bricks they feel strongly about, and they do everything they can to ensure those beliefs are passed down to the next generation. If these early beliefs were handed to you by someone you trusted, those bricks are probably holding a foundational place in your house of faith.

For instance, my great-grandmother grew up Southern Baptist. For her, abstaining from alcohol and dancing with boys was a foundational brick, right alongside the resurrection of Jesus Christ. She didn't come up with this belief system on her own,

1. Isabel Fattal, "Why So Many Americans Have Stopped Going to Church," *Atlantic*, August 3, 2023, https://www.theatlantic.com/newsletters/archive/2023/08/why-church-religion-attendance-decline/674916.

and she certainly didn't read it in the Bible. She was taught it by people she trusted, who felt strongly about it, and it was reinforced in her community.

Whether or not we grew up in church, we've all been through a construction phase to some extent. But somewhere along the way, we begin to have questions about one or more of those bricks; something we believe bumps up against something we learn or experience, and we find ourselves unable to reconcile the two.

This happens for all sorts of reasons. For my great-grandmother, it was attending a high school dance and realizing that she didn't spontaneously combust while doing the Charleston with a boy from her homeroom class. For me, it happened when a pastor I grew up admiring was arrested for abuse.

When our lived experiences contradict the beliefs we've been given, we are faced with a choice: ignore our experience and believe what we've always believed or make a change to our house of faith. The latter forces us to take the brick out of its place, hold it up for examination, and decide whether we want to put it back, throw it away, or replace it with something better.

This process, called "deconstruction," is a universal experience. What isn't universal are the unique decisions each of us faces with every brick we examine and how we choose to move forward with our own house of faith.

Some evangelical leaders assert that people deconstruct so they can sin more freely and feel justified while doing so,[2] because they are being held captive by Satan,[3] or because it's the

2. Josh Butler, "4 Causes of Deconstruction," The Gospel Coalition, November 9, 2021, https://www.thegospelcoalition.org/article/4-causes-deconstruction.

3. Alisa Childers and Tim Barnett, "Help! My Loved One Is Deconstructing," The Gospel Coalition, February 17, 2024, https://www.thegospelcoalition.org/article/help-loved-one-deconstructing.

"sexy thing to do."[4] But in my experience, people don't deconstruct because it's "sexy" or because they're looking for excuses to sin. They do it because the Christianity they've encountered is so unlike Christ.

I've talked to hundreds of people about this and have yet to encounter anyone who voluntarily chose to start deconstructing, myself included. No one wakes up one morning, pours a cup of coffee, and randomly declares, "Today I'm going to question everything I've ever been taught!" Deconstruction is involuntary; it happens when something we've been taught to believe comes into conflict with something we experience. For example:

- We were taught that Christians fight against abuse, but then we watched church leaders at the highest level cover up abuse and enable abusers time and time again.
- We were taught that Christians value ethics and morals, but then we watched many Christian leaders wholly support a political leader who openly mocks disabled folks, brags about sexual assault, calls migrants "animals," lies constantly, and was found liable of rape, among other things.[5]

4. Matt Chandler, "The Depth of the Gospel," sermon, Village Church, August 29, 2021, Flower Mound, TX, available at https://youtu.be/X_r8IMU647g.

5. "Donald Trump Under Fire for Mocking Disabled Reporter," *BBC*, November 26, 2015, https://www.bbc.com/news/world-us-canada-34930042; "Donald Trump *Access Hollywood* Tape," Wikipedia, last modified October 2, 2024, https://en.wikipedia.org/wiki/Donald_Trump_Access_Hollywood_tape; Nathan Layne, Gram Slattery, and Tim Reid, "Trump Calls Migrants 'Animals,' Intensifying Focus on Illegal Immigration," *Reuters*, April 3, 2024, https://www.reuters.com/world/us/trump-expected-highlight-murder-michigan-woman-immigration-speech-2024-04-02; Glenn Kessler, Salvador Rizzo, and Meg Kelly, "Trump's False or Misleading Claims Total 30,573 over 4 Years," *Washington Post*, January 24, 2021, https://www.washingtonpost.com/politics/2021/01/24/trumps-false-or-misleading-claims-total-30573-over-four-years; Aaron Blake, "Judge Clarifies: Yes, Trump Was Found to Have Raped E. Jean Carroll," *Washington Post*, July 19, 2023, https://www.washingtonpost.com/politics/2023/07/19/trump-carroll-judge-rape.

- We were taught that Christians welcome everyone into God's family, but then we watched LGBTQ+ folks who were diligently following Jesus get kicked out of various church communities.
- We were taught that Christians are called to be generous, but then we saw pastor after pastor get caught embezzling money.
- We were taught that Christians hate racism, but then we watched many of them post "all lives matter" after George Floyd's murder.
- We were taught that Christians abhor violence, but then we read polls showing they support torture at higher rates than those who are nonreligious.[6]
- We were taught that Christians strive for peace, but then we watched an insurrection led by people carrying signs bearing the name of Jesus.
- We were taught that Christians care for the vulnerable, but then we heard pastors preach that people experiencing homelessness are lazy addicts.
- We were taught that Christians take care of the sick, but then we watched prominent pastors call the COVID-19 virus fake news and host what ended up being superspreader events.

All these things and more leave many folks feeling like the only Christlike option is to disentangle their faith from these harmful beliefs and behaviors. I'm grateful so many people are

6. Sarah Posner, "Christians More Supportive of Torture Than Non-Religious Americans," *Religion Dispatches*, December 16, 2014, https://religiondispatches.org/christians-more-supportive-of-torture-than-non-religious-americans; and "The Religious Dimensions of the Torture Debate," Pew Research Center, April 29, 2009, updated May 7, 2009, https://www.pewresearch.org/religion/2009/04/29/the-religious-dimensions-of-the-torture-debate.

choosing to reexamine, deconstruct, and reconstruct. Thank God so many folks have stopped pretending nothing is wrong! Thank God they refuse to enable these abuses any longer! Even former Southern Baptist pastor and denominational leader Russell Moore understands this truth. Speaking about folks who have deconstructed, he says:

> The culture often does not reject us because they don't believe the church's doctrinal and moral teachings, but because they have evidence that the *church* doesn't believe its own doctrinal and moral teachings. They suspect that Jesus is just a means to an end—to some political agenda, to a market for selling merchandise, or for the predatory appetites of some maniacal narcissist.[7]
>
> Not one of them walked away because they wanted to curry favor with "elites" or because they wanted to rebel. If anything, the posture of many of these people was not that of the Prodigal Son off in the far country so much as that of his father, waiting by the road for a prodigal they loved and wanted to embrace again: their church.[8]

Actor, comedian, and former conservative evangelical Rhett McLaughlin puts it even more bluntly: "Your kids are not leaving the church because you didn't train them enough. Your kids are leaving the church because you trained them well enough to develop a sense for truth and justice. You let them read the words of Jesus, and they got it, and they've recognized that the church doesn't seem to be interested in those words. They're

7. Russell Moore, "Enraged by Ravi (Part 1): The Wreckage of Ravi Zacharias," *Russell Moore* (blog), February 15, 2021, https://www.russellmoore.com/2021/02/15/enraged-by-ravi-part-1-the-wreckage-of-ravi-zacharias.

8. Russell Moore, "My Dad Taught Me How to Love the Exvangelical," *Christianity Today*, October 21, 2021, https://www.christianitytoday.com/ct/2021/october-web-only/russell-moore-dad-taught-love-exvangelical-pastor-church.html.

not leaving because they don't know the truth; they're leaving because they do."[9]

I am more convinced every day that if the church in America cares at all about stemming the tide of people fleeing Christianity, we need to do a whole lot less shaming of doubters and a whole lot more shepherding of people through their deconstruction. We also need to shift away from a text-centered faith to a Jesus-centered faith.

Reconstructing a Jesus-Centered Faith

Far too often, we've asked the Bible—every single verse, from Genesis to Revelation—to be the foundation of our faith. Yet if Christianity is built on the foundation that every word of the Bible is to be read literally, our entire faith begins to crumble very quickly for some of the reasons we explored in chapter 3.

We don't have a text-centered faith. We have a Jesus-centered faith. You may be thinking, "How do you know that, Zach?" Good question! Because the Bible tells me so. Look at the very beginning of John's account of Jesus's life: "In the beginning was the Word, and the Word was with God, and the Word was God. He was with God in the beginning. Through him all things were made; without him nothing was made that has been made. In him was life, and that life was the light of all mankind. The light shines in the darkness, and the darkness has not overcome it" (John 1:1–5).

Then John 1:14 says, "The Word was written down on scrolls and given to us." Wait . . . that's not what it says. Here's what John actually wrote: "The Word became flesh and made his dwelling among us."

9. "Rhett's Spiritual Deconstruction," *Ear Biscuits* (podcast), episode 226, February 3, 2020, available at https://youtu.be/1qbna6t1bzw.

When God wanted to give his Word to the world he created, he didn't write a book. Instead, he became a person. Jesus is God in the flesh. God with skin on. This truth should transform our Bibles from the center of our faith to just one of the primary ways we learn about the true center of our faith—Jesus Christ.

The Bible is like the star the magi follow in order to find Jesus after he is born in Bethlehem. The Bible is like John the Baptist, who says, "Look, the Lamb of God, who takes away the sin of the world!" (John 1:29). The Bible points us to Jesus, not the other way around. Far too often, we have elevated the book above the main character. Some might note here that we know about this main character only because of the Bible, but it's actually the other way around: We don't know about Jesus because of the Bible; we know about the Bible because of the resurrection of Jesus.

Jesus was born to a scandalized mom from a low-class family in a town with a bad reputation.[10] He didn't write any books, he didn't compose any songs, and he never traveled more than a hundred miles from his birthplace. So how is he the founder of the largest religion in the world? Because of a library of books compiled four hundred years after his recorded death? No! Because he lived radically, taught boldly, predicted he was going to die and come back to life, and then he did.

Christianity did not begin when someone read something. Christianity began when someone saw something: the resurrected Jesus. This fundamental reality should change the way we read and relate to the Bible, as well as how we construct, deconstruct, and reconstruct our house of faith. If anything in our house of faith contradicts the words or works of Jesus, we must choose Jesus. When we take out each brick and examine it,

10. "Philip found Nathanael and told him, 'We have found the one Moses wrote about in the Law, and about whom the prophets also wrote—Jesus of Nazareth, the son of Joseph.' 'Nazareth! Can anything good come from there?' Nathanael asked" (John 1:45–46).

Jesus must be the filter through which we decide what to keep and what to throw away.

Six times in the Sermon on the Mount, Jesus says, "You have heard that it was said . . . but I tell you . . ." And each time, he pushes back on a commonly held belief of the day. For example, "You have heard that it was said, 'Love your neighbor and hate your enemy.' But I tell you, love your enemies and pray for those who persecute you" (Matt. 5:43–44). In the book of 2 Kings, Elijah calls fire down from heaven on his enemies, but Jesus says we are supposed to love our enemies and pray for them. So should we hate our enemies, or should we love them? I'm going to do what Jesus told me to do. Because the Bible isn't what I'm following; Jesus is. I'm not a "little Bible"; I'm a "little Christ."

When we strip the Bible of its context, culture, and original intent and we ignore the leading of the Holy Spirit, we can make the Bible say just about anything we want it to say. We can use it to support things that directly contradict Jesus and God's kingdom. Satan himself demonstrates this when he uses Scripture to tempt Jesus to sin (Luke 4:1–13).

Christians spend so much time arguing about what is "biblical" and "unbiblical" when we really should be distinguishing between what is Christlike and what is un-Christlike. Writer Jordan Harrell says it like this: "Genocide is biblical. Loving your enemy is biblical. But only one is Christlike. Slavery is biblical. Chainbreaking is biblical. But only one is Christlike. Patriarchy is biblical. Counter-cultural elevation of women is biblical. But only one is Christlike. Retributive violence is biblical. Grace-filled restoration is biblical. But only one is Christlike. Segregation is biblical. Unity is biblical. But only one is Christlike. Christ transforms, not the Bible."[11]

11. Jordan Harrell (@jordanharrellwriter), "This one has floated around a bit and I feel the need to clarify," Instagram, April 28, 2024, https://www.instagram.com/p/C6T-TiArx-u.

To borrow a line from Brian Zahnd: Jesus is what God has to say.[12] Jesus is the fullest revelation we have of who God is. For Christians, the entirety of the Bible centers on a person and a series of events—the incarnation, life, death, and resurrection of Jesus Christ. One of my favorite verses in the Bible is where Jesus chastises those who elevate Scripture above him: "You search the Scriptures because you think they give you eternal life. But the Scriptures point to me! Yet you refuse to come to me to receive this life" (John 5:39–40 NLT).

We must interpret all of Scripture through the lens of Jesus.[13] This means that if something in Scripture seemingly contradicts the person, work, or teachings of Jesus, we have misunderstood, misinterpreted, or misapplied it. Theologian James Cone makes it plain: "All Christian doctrines must be interpreted in the light of Jesus Christ."[14]

The New Testament teaches that Jesus is fully God in the flesh. Fully human, but also fully divine. Paul says it like this: "For in Christ lives all the fullness of God in a human body" (Col. 2:9 NLT). Or as the late translator J. B. Phillips says, "The historic Christian doctrine of the divinity of Christ does not simply mean that Jesus is like God. It is far more radical than that. It means that if we want to know what God is like, we should look at Jesus. God is Christlike!"[15]

12. Brian Zahnd, "Jesus Is What God Has to Say," *Brian Zahnd* (blog), February 12, 2015, https://brianzahnd.com/2015/02/jesus-god-say.

13. This is not a radical or progressive claim. In fact, the Southern Baptist Convention's own statement of faith declared the same thing until it was removed by a committee more committed to a literalism lens than to Jesus: "The criterion by which the Bible is to be interpreted is Jesus Christ." This language was removed in the 2000 version of The Baptist Faith and Message. Southern Baptist Convention, Baptist Faith and Message 1963, "I. Scriptures," May 9, 1963, https://www.midwaybc.net/wp-content/uploads/2020/01/baptist-faith-message-1963.pdf.

14. James H. Cone, "The Doctrine of Man in the Theology of Karl Barth" (PhD diss., Garrett-Evangelical Theological Seminary, 1959), 158.

15. J. B. Phillips, *Your God Is Too Small* (Macmillan, 1961), 93.

If Jesus is the fullest picture we have of who God is and what God is like, that should change how we understand Scripture. That is to say, we need to put on our Jesus lens when we read the Bible.

What Does Jesus Care About?

Practically, reading the Bible through the Jesus lens starts with understanding what Jesus cares about. Jesus is asked 183 questions in Scripture. Do you know how many he answers directly? Three. And when Jesus is asked a question, he often responds with questions of his own. If we combine those with the questions Jesus is asked, we get 307 questions.

If you're keeping track, that's 307 questions asked, 183 questions received, and only 3 answers given.[16] Jesus is curious. If we want to use the Jesus lens when interpreting Scripture, we must also embody a posture of humble curiosity rather than arrogant assuredness. Additionally, if we want to understand who Jesus is and what he came to earth to do and be, those three answers he gave are probably important.

The first of three answers comes when the disciples aren't able to heal a young boy. The boy's father later brings his son to Jesus, who heals him immediately. The disciples are understandably frustrated, so they ask Jesus why they couldn't heal the kid themselves. Here is Jesus's answer: "Because you have so little faith. Truly I tell you, if you have faith as small as a mustard seed, you can say to this mountain, 'Move from here to there,' and it will move. Nothing will be impossible for you" (Matt. 17:20).

Jesus doesn't say the disciples couldn't heal the young boy because they lacked knowledge, qualification, or power. He says it was because they lacked faith. What is "faith"? This is a vital

16. Martin B. Copenhaver, *Jesus Is the Question: The 307 Questions Jesus Asked and the Three He Answered* (Abingdon, 2014).

question because Christians usually equate faith with a set of doctrines we believe. Rather than a focus on following Jesus, we often reduce Christianity to doctrines, dogmas, and belief statements.

When people ask if you are a Christian, often what they are asking is "Do you believe all the things I've deemed necessary for Christians to believe, and do you believe them in the same way I do?" But that is an incredibly recent and, I think, an incredibly shallow understanding of the Christian faith.

Jesus doesn't say, "Here is the truth; believe it." He says, "I am the truth; follow me" (see John 14:6). Being a Christian is not primarily about checking all the right doctrinal boxes or defending the correct dogmas. Being a Christian is about following the way of Jesus. In his book *The Sin of Certainty*, Bible scholar Peter Enns puts it like this: "The life of Christian faith is more than agreeing with a set of beliefs about Christ, morality, or how to read the Bible. It means being so intimately connected to Christ that his crucifixion is ours, his death is our death, and his life is our life—which is hardly something we can grasp with our minds. It has to be experienced."[17]

Faith is something we both embody and experience, as well as intellectually assent to. It is more than belief; it is a posture—a way of living and moving in the world. A shallow understanding of faith also comes with the unintended consequence of setting faith and doubt in opposition to each other. If faith is absolute certainty about our beliefs, then any doubts or questions become an attack on faith.

But the opposite of faith isn't doubt. In fact, I believe the opposite of faith is certainty. If I'm absolutely sure about everything I believe, then placing my faith in God and choosing to trust Jesus become unnecessary. Faith isn't unquestioning belief

17. Peter Enns, *The Sin of Certainty: Why God Desires Our Trust More Than Our "Correct" Beliefs* (HarperCollins, 2016), 162.

in a set of doctrines. Faith is trusting God and God's love with everything:

our questions
our doubts
our anger
our changing beliefs
our deconstruction
our reconstruction
our broken selves
our broken situations
our big, broken world

Putting on the Jesus lens means being open about our doubts, wrestling with our uncertainties, and working out our faith alongside Jesus and our communities. It also means we can find comfort in knowing that we'll never have everything figured out and that questions and doubts are an inevitable part of a living and growing faith.

The second question Jesus answers directly comes when Peter asks him about forgiveness: "'Lord, how many times shall I forgive my brother or sister who sins against me? Up to seven times?' Jesus answered, 'I tell you, not seven times, but seventy-seven times'" (Matt. 18:21–22).

Peter is one of Jesus's closest disciples, and he ends up leading the church in Jerusalem. He asks this question because he has seen Jesus preaching and practicing forgiveness in ways that blow his mind. So Peter is like "Okay, Jesus, I know you keep talking about forgiveness, but how much is too much? When do we stop forgiving?" At face value, it looks like Jesus is just playing on words in order to demonstrate that we are supposed to keep on forgiving forever, and that's partially true, but there's more to it than that. Jesus is actually referring to a passage from the book of Genesis about a guy named Lamech.

Lamech is a descendant of Cain, the man who murdered his brother Abel in cold blood, and he carries on Cain's legacy in a major way. Lamech is so violent and vindictive that he writes a song about all the terrible things he's done. Here's what he says: "I have killed a man for wounding me, a young man for injuring me. If Cain is avenged seven times, then Lamech seventy-seven times" (Gen. 4:23–24).

The people listening to Peter and Jesus that day would have immediately gotten this reference. Jesus is declaring, in no uncertain terms, that the kingdom of God is never going back to the way of Lamech. Lamech was all about unrelenting revenge, but Jesus is all about unrelenting forgiveness. No matter who we are, what we've done, or where our journey has taken us, God's forgiveness is available to us through the work of Jesus.

So Jesus answers one question about faith and one about forgiveness. While the first two are great, the third and final answer is the best by far. Jesus is asked by a fellow expert in religious law what the greatest commandment is. If we modernized this question, it would sound something like "What does God say is the most important thing for us to do?"

Jesus not only answers this question directly but also answers it so decisively that his words have come to define what it means to be a Christian more than any other verse in the Bible. Here's what he says: "'You must love the Lord your God with all your heart, all your soul, and all your mind.' This is the first and greatest commandment. A second is equally important: 'Love your neighbor as yourself.' The entire law and all the demands of the prophets are based on these two commandments" (Matt. 22:37–40 NLT).

It doesn't get more direct than that. Jesus commands us to love God and love others; that's what is most important. He even doubles down on just how far-reaching this commandment is; he says that "all the Law and the Prophets" find their full expression here. This is Jesus saying that everything God has ever commanded comes down to these two directives. Like a door hangs on two hinges, the entirety of the Christian life hangs on loving God and loving others.

It's worth noting here that Jesus emphasizes the importance of sacrificially loving others not once but twice during his final time of teaching with his closest followers:

> A new command I give you: Love one another. As I have loved you, so you must love one another. By this everyone will know that you are my disciples, if you love one another. (John 13:34–35)

> My command is this: Love each other as I have loved you. Greater love has no one than this: to lay down one's life for one's friends. . . . This is my command: Love each other. (John 15:12–13, 17)

I love the way Beth Moore says it: "Love God. Love one another. Love your neighbor. Love your enemy. That about covers it. In Christ's meticulous census, the community exempt from the love of Christians has a population of exactly zero."[18] Interpreting the Bible through the Jesus lens with love as our guide is not a new concept. In the fourth century, Saint Augustine of Hippo, in one of the earliest theological texts devoted to biblical interpretation, writes, "Whoever, then, thinks that he understands the Holy Scriptures, or any part of them, but puts such an interpretation upon them as does not tend to build up this twofold love of God and our neighbour, does not yet understand them as he ought."[19]

18. Beth Moore, *Chasing Vines: Finding Your Way to an Immensely Fruitful Life* (Tyndale, 2020), 260.

19. Augustine, *On Christian Doctrine* 1.36, https://www.ccel.org/ccel/augustine/doctrine.xxxvi.html.

If we are interpreting the Bible in ways that do not yield more love of God and neighbor, the two things Jesus says are most important, then we are interpreting it incorrectly. Sacrificial love isn't just about how we interpret Scripture, it's also how we live our lives. This is the faith we've been handed by Christians who have come before us.

In the year AD 125, a Greek philosopher named Aristides attempted to explain Christianity to Roman emperor Hadrian. Here's how he described these early Christians: "Falsehood is not found among them; and they love one another, and from widows they do not turn away their esteem; and they deliver the orphan from him who treats him harshly. And he, who has, gives to him who has not, without boasting. And when they see a stranger, they take him in to their homes and rejoice over him as a very brother; for they do not call them brethren after the flesh, but brethren after the spirit and in God."[20]

These communities were so radical in their love that even the Greek philosophers and the occupying Roman government were impressed by them. If the ancient church was known for its sacrificial love, then the modern church should be too. Jesus cared about a lot of things, but love was always at the top of the list. Putting on the Jesus lens means interpreting Scripture in ways that lead to love.

When multiple interpretive options exist—and they almost always do—we must choose the interpretation that most closely aligns with the person, work, and teachings of Jesus Christ, which looks like sacrificial love for all people. As Paul says, "The greatest of these is love" (1 Cor. 13:13). Anything else is un-Christian.

20. Aristides, *Apology* 15, trans. D. M. Kay, Early Christian Writings, accessed January 8, 2025, https://www.earlychristianwritings.com/text/aristides-kay.html.

8

the context lens

"The One Who Seeks Will Find"

> The notion that we read the New Testament exactly as the early Christians did, without any weight of tradition coloring our interpretation, is an illusion. It is also a dangerous illusion, for it tends to absolutize our interpretation, confusing it with the Word of God.
>
> —Justo González, *The Story of Christianity*

I met my first love in a sixth-grade English class. I was so disruptive that my teacher moved my desk into the corner of the room and then put a trifold gym mat around me so I couldn't see anything except the wall. The classmate seated closest to me was a girl named Amy.

Amy was a compliant, straight-A student who was a faithful member of her youth group and beloved by every adult at the school. I was not. I was a punk kid who'd been kicked out of both a church youth group and a private Christian school in just the previous year alone. The very next year, as a seventh grader, I would set the record for office referrals and lunch detentions.

In case you're wondering, I received thirty-seven office referrals and over one hundred lunch detentions. According to my sources at the middle school, no one has ever come close to those numbers. I'm the Wayne Gretzky of preteen troublemakers. No one is catching that record.

Amy and I had most of our classes together that year, and I always ended up sitting next to her, mostly because I would get in trouble and be moved away from the other hooligans and next to the most exemplary student in class. Throughout middle school, we were in puppy love, but her dad had an unyielding rule: no dating until she was sixteen. When her family decided to move after our seventh-grade year, I was distraught. But then, on the last day of school, we made a promise: I would be her first "real date" after she turned sixteen.

For the next four years, we kept up through AIM (that's AOL Instant Messenger for all you Gen Z folks), and when her sixteenth birthday finally rolled around, I took Amy out for her first date. I thought it went well! She did not. That's because we had taken seemingly inevitable divergent paths since that promise at the end of seventh grade. I spent most of my time partying and playing sports, while she was a leader in her youth group and on track to graduate early as the salutatorian.

Amy knew we were headed in different directions and that dating me wasn't exactly a wise choice, so when I texted her after the date, "Let's hang out again soon!" she politely replied, "Maybe just as friends :)."

We didn't see each other much over the next year, but when the summer before my senior year of high school and her freshman year of college came around, we were brought together by God or fate or some combination of the two. One night, while I was out on the lake with some friends, I overdosed on a combination of cough medicine and alcohol. The next night, I was back on the water trying to pretend nothing had happened when I witnessed a college student overdose and drown right in front of me. We tried to pull him out of the water, but couldn't get to him in time.

Needless to say, I was shaken up. After that experience, I began to struggle with some existential questions:

Why am I here?
What is the purpose of life?
Is God real?

Even though I'd been kicked out of church and found the Christianity I'd been exposed to archaic and oppressive, I decided to try again. Lo and behold, I fell in love with Jesus. But I had no idea what to do or whom to tell about it. Then it hit me: "I have to call Amy!" She was the only Christian I'd ever known who didn't judge me or beat me over the head with a Bible.

So I invited her to lunch at Cracker Barrel (quite possibly the Whitest thing I've ever done), where we ended up spending hours together that day, just talking about life and Jesus and everything in between. I told her about all the terrible things I had been doing—a laundry list of sins that might have caused even the tax collectors and prostitutes of Jesus's day to blush. I half expected her to stand up and politely excuse herself from my unholy presence, but she didn't.

Amy treated me exactly like the Jesus I read about treated people. And just like I fell in love with his love, I began to fall in love with hers as well. There is so much more to the rest of the story, but the short version is this: We started dating a few weeks later, got married when we were twenty-one, had our first child when we were twenty-five, started Restore when we were twenty-six, and just celebrated fifteen years of marriage.

We've been through so much together: foster care, church planting, deconstruction, reconstruction, the highest of highs, and the lowest of lows. Through it all, she has been the rock of our family. She's taught me so much about what it means to have faith and what it looks like to follow Jesus. I'm honestly not sure I'd be a Christian without Amy, much less a pastor.

So when I started working in pastoral ministry as a nineteen-year-old college sophomore and saw the way women are often treated in the church, I was really confused. I could preach, but Amy couldn't, even though she was exponentially more qualified. I could lead, but she couldn't, even though she had a decade more of church experience than I did. Even though I'm far more emotionally driven, she was the one who was stereotyped as hysterical anytime she showed passion. My comments about the Bible were taken as authoritative, while hers were dismissed out of hand, even though she had memorized more Scripture than I'd ever even read.

I was confused and unsettled and shocked. But you know who wasn't any of those things? Amy. Because that's how the church had treated her and other women her entire life: as second-class citizens. The subjugation of women, often under the banner of "biblical womanhood," is tragically prevalent in the modern church.

Sexism is a unique problem because it's the only kind of marginalization that affects the majority of church members. All the other "isms" we often talk about come down to a majority-versus-minority problem. This happens with racial minorities, sexual minorities, religious minorities, and so on. But sexism is something that affects more than half of the church. According to the latest data from the Pew Research Center:

- Women are 12 percent more likely to say their faith is "very important" in their lives than men.

- They are 10 percent more likely to read and study the Bible.
- They are 9 percent more likely to attend weekly services.[1]

In addition, the average church membership is about 61 percent women and 39 percent men, which means there are about thirteen million more adult women in church than men on any given Sunday.[2]

And yet, even as the majority sex, women are often marginalized in the church. So how did this happen? In her game-changing book, *The Making of Biblical Womanhood: How the Subjugation of Women Became Gospel Truth*, historian and professor Beth Allison Barr goes into great detail about how we got here.

The subjugation of women was called "biblical womanhood" not because of Scripture but because patriarchy has been the predominant worldview of most cultures throughout most of history. And just as people did with slavery and genocide and other terrible things, they snatched a few Bible verses out of context and held them up as proof that their oppression and violence were ordained by God. This is what it means to take the Lord's name in vain. It's not about saying "Oh my god!" when you're frustrated, although I still get onto my kids about that. Taking the Lord's name in vain is about using God to justify subjugation and marginalization, it's about validating violence with Bible verses, and it's about calling yourself a Christian without doing the work of Christ—justice, liberation, and love.

1. "Gender Composition," 2014 Religious Landscape Study, Pew Research Center, https://www.pewresearch.org/religious-landscape-study/database/gender-composition.

2. David Murrow, "Quick Facts on Christianity's Gender Gap," *David Murrow* (blog), June 15, 2021, https://davidmurrow.com/quick-facts-on-christianitys-gender-gap.

As the saying goes, I can do all things through a verse taken out of context. When we approach issues like sexism in the church, we have to go deeper than a verse here and there. We must look at both the passages in question and the entire biblical narrative in context. The context lens is vitally important if we are looking for better ways to read the Bible.

As I said earlier, none of us belong to the intended audience of Scripture. We aren't the original audience, we don't speak the original languages, and we don't live in the original geographical and cultural settings. This all means we don't intrinsically understand the biblical context, so we must do everything we can to understand the various aspects of it—things like culture, author, audience, purpose, language, and genre. As biblical scholar Justo González says, "The notion that we read the New Testament exactly as the early Christians did, without any weight of tradition coloring our interpretation, is an illusion. It is also a dangerous illusion, for it tends to absolutize our interpretation, confusing it with the Word of God."[3]

González is absolutely right. Reading the Bible out of context while pretending that we have no biases is a dangerous proposition because it often leads to incredibly harmful interpretations. I had a seminary professor who used to repeat the quip "A text without context is a pretext for a proof text." Proof texting is using a verse or passage to prop up an ideology that Jesus and the whole of Scripture don't actually support. This is how bigotry gets baptized.

"I Do Not Permit a Woman to Teach"

Two verses in particular have been taken out of context and used to oppress women. One is used to subjugate women in the

3. Justo L. González, *Santa Biblia: The Bible Through Hispanic Eyes* (Abingdon, 1996), 13.

church, and the other is used to subjugate women in the home. The first one is 1 Timothy 2:12: "I do not permit a woman to teach or to assume authority over a man; she must be quiet." This is the only verse in the entire Bible that seemingly places any kind of restriction on women preaching, teaching, or pastoring. Meanwhile, both the Old Testament and the New Testament are filled with examples of women preaching, teaching, and pastoring.

I was an eighteen-year-old college student when I first learned those realities. I was raised in the Southern Baptist Convention, which upholds heavy restrictions on what women can and cannot do—restrictions I had rarely questioned. Some of that was because I was a man who was privileged not to feel those restrictions directly, and some of it was because I was fairly uninterested in anything related to church until I was seventeen. My journey of untangling sexism from my faith began in a freshman New Testament class, in which my professor challenged us to simply look at the women depicted in Scripture to see if their lives matched what we'd been told women were "allowed" to do. What I found is exactly what Beth Allison Barr says so succinctly: "Biblical women contradict modern ideas of biblical womanhood."[4] Who are some examples? I'm so glad you asked.

Deborah is a prophet placed in leadership over God's people in Judges 4. She is a judge, which means she is the point leader of Israel for forty years.

Huldah is a prophet and an expert in the Torah, which comprises the first five books in our Bible—Genesis, Exodus, Leviticus, Numbers, and Deuteronomy. She interprets it and authorizes the canonization of the core of the Jewish Scriptures in 2 Kings 22.

4. Beth Allison Barr, *The Making of Biblical Womanhood: How the Subjugation of Women Became Gospel Truth* (Brazos, 2021), 11.

Esther is the queen and liberator of God's people. She bravely faces the possibility of death to save an entire nation from genocide. Her story is found in the book that bears her name.

Hagar is the first person to give God a name. In Genesis 16, she calls God "El Roi," which means "the God who sees me." Prior to this interaction, God was the one sharing God's name with humanity. Hagar is a single mother and a slave with no rights or privileges whatsoever, but she gives God a name and God accepts it.

Mary of Nazareth (the mother of Jesus) is the first person to have the Messiah revealed to her. She is also the first person to believe Jesus is who he says he is and to become a disciple (Luke 1).

Elizabeth is the first person to prophesy over Jesus while he is inside the womb (Luke 1). She is Mary's cousin and the mother of John the Baptist.

Anna is the first person to prophesy over Jesus after he is born (Luke 2). When Mary and Joseph take Jesus to the temple, they meet the prophet Anna, who says that Jesus will bring redemption to humanity.

Mary of Bethany is the first person to anoint Jesus as king (Matt. 26).

The Samaritan woman, who meets Jesus at the well in John 4, becomes the first evangelist. She believes that Jesus is the Messiah, and he sends her back to her town to preach about him; many of the people there come to believe in Jesus because of her words.

Mary Magdalene is not only a disciple of Jesus but also the first gospel preacher. In John 20, she is the first to see the resurrected Jesus, and he commissions her to share this good news with all the other disciples.

Lydia decides to follow Jesus in Acts 16. In addition to becoming a pastor and evangelist, Lydia is the first church planter in Europe.

Junia is one of only two people in Scripture deemed "outstanding among the apostles" (Rom. 16:7). Junia isn't just an apostle; she is one of the most esteemed. How do we know that? Because another apostle named Paul tells us about Junia in his letter to the church in Rome.

Phoebe is trusted with the sacred task of delivering, presenting, and answering questions about Paul's letter to the Roman church. She is another pastor and leader in the early church. Paul calls her "sister" (Rom. 16:1), which elevates her to status of peer with Paul and says that she has been a ministry provider for him and other pastors as well.

Priscilla is another good friend and co-laborer of Paul. She is known not only for being a pastor but also for correcting the theology of a prominent male pastor named Apollos.

Nympha, Euodia, and Syntyche are three more women Paul mentions by name who pastor churches in their homes.

Now, depending on your spiritual background or church tradition, you might be a little confused. Isn't Paul the one who tells women to be quiet in church and never have authority over men? Isn't he the one who says women shouldn't be pastors or preachers?

Well, no. He doesn't say those things—not in the universalizing way we often read him. What Paul does do is address a specific issue inside a specific church. And that is where 1 Timothy 2:12 comes in. One important and easy-to-implement practice when using the context lens is to simply read the passage surrounding any given verse. We can't understand 1 Timothy 2 if we don't understand 1 Timothy 1. Here is how this letter begins:

> Paul, an apostle of Christ Jesus by the command of God our Savior and of Christ Jesus our hope, to Timothy my true son in the faith: Grace, mercy and peace from God the Father and Christ Jesus our Lord. As I urged you when I went into Macedonia, stay there in Ephesus so that you may command certain people not to teach false doctrines any longer or to devote themselves to myths and endless genealogies. Such things promote controversial speculations rather than advancing God's work—which is by faith. The goal of this command is love, which comes from a pure heart and a good conscience and a sincere faith. Some have departed from these and have turned to meaningless talk. They want to be teachers of the law, but they do not know what they are talking about or what they so confidently affirm. (1:1–7)

This letter is written to Timothy for a very specific reason: False teachers are leading people away from Jesus in the Ephesian church. They are not promoting faith and love, the two most important things. "They want to be teachers . . . , but they do not know what they are talking about."

This is the singular point of this letter: Timothy is tasked with combating false teachers and false teachings in the church in Ephesus. Chapter 2 begins to outline what that should look like. Here is the full passage in context, including the infamous verse 12:

> Therefore I want the men everywhere to pray, lifting up holy hands without anger or disputing. I also want the women to dress modestly, with decency and propriety, adorning themselves, not with elaborate hairstyles or gold or pearls or expensive clothes, but with good deeds, appropriate for women who profess to worship God. A woman should learn in quietness and full submission. I do not permit a woman to teach or to assume authority over a man; she must be quiet. For Adam was formed first, then Eve. And Adam was not the one deceived; it was the woman who

> was deceived and became a sinner. But women will be saved through childbearing—if they continue in faith, love and holiness with propriety. (2:8–15)

These verses come with a myriad of interpretive options, as this has been one of the most highly disputed passages in church history. But using the context lens means understanding it as a part of the larger subject matter of Paul's letter. When we do this, the best interpretive option becomes clear: These verses are addressing specific false teachers and false teachings. Biblical scholars have surmised the following:

- There were men who were using prayer inappropriately, so Timothy needed to require all the men in the Ephesian church to lift their hands when they prayed.
- There were women flaunting their wealth by dressing immodestly, so Timothy was given very specific instructions on how those women should dress.
- And finally, there was a female false teacher who was claiming authority over a specific man in the Ephesian church, and she needed to be corrected.

Notice that verses 11 and 12 are the only verses that use singular nouns: "*A woman* should learn in quietness and full submission. I do not permit *a woman* to teach or to assume authority over a man; she must be quiet." So a strong interpretive option, considering both the context of this passage and the other writings of the New Testament, is that there was *one* female false teacher who was claiming authority over a specific man in the Ephesian church, and Timothy was told to put a stop to it.

It's impossible to know the exact situation being addressed with this false teacher since we are so far removed from it, but

I do believe we can unmistakably know what this passage does not mean:

- It does not mean that all men everywhere are required to lift up their hands when they pray—no one practiced it then, and no one practices it now, and there is no other reference to that being a requirement for prayer anywhere else in the Bible.
- It does not mean that women cannot teach and must be quiet in church—again, no one practiced this then. As I outline above, Paul sends arguably his most important letter (Romans) with a deacon named Phoebe, and she taught the contents of his letter to the church in Rome.
- Last, it does not mean that only women who give birth will be saved—that makes no sense and contradicts everything the New Testament teaches about salvation.

No one, including the staunchest patriarchal pastor, interprets this passage literally. So why do people interpret verse 12 literally? Because of sexism. Plain and simple. There is no other reason to literalize verse 12 and then contextualize verses 8, 9, 10, 11, 13, 14, and 15, unless one is looking for biblical rationale to subjugate women in the church.

Paul is addressing specific issues in a specific church. Yet some folks have taken those specific instructions about specific issues among a specific group of people and said that they apply everywhere and for all time. In other words, they've taken something meant to be descriptive and made it prescriptive.

This happens a lot with the Bible. Did you know Paul also tells women to wear a head covering? Did you know he tells Christians to "greet each other with a holy kiss" when they meet? But no one is advocating for a prescriptive understanding of those passages. Contrary to what you may have been told, Paul honored, valued, and labored alongside women throughout his ministry. As the most prominent church leader in the first-century world, he leaned on, learned from, and considered himself in equal partnership with a number of women when it came to the work of Jesus.

"Wives, Submit to Your Husbands"

At this point, you might be thinking, "Okay, Zach. All of that might be true, but it's also true that Paul plainly says, 'Wives, submit yourselves to your own husbands as you do to the Lord.' You can't wiggle your way out of that one."

And you're right. Paul says exactly that in Ephesians 5:22. This is the verse most often used to subjugate women in the home, in their relationships, and in society more broadly. But again, we have to look at it in context. And we don't need to read all of Ephesians to understand the context. In fact, we don't even have to read the whole chapter! Just look at the verse immediately preceding: "Submit to one another out of reverence for Christ" (5:21).

Paul is teaching mutual submission, not one-sided subjugation. Paul goes on to give instructions for how husbands should submit, how wives should submit, and how children should submit. What is so radical about this passage of Scripture, when we understand the context, is that Paul is mimicking the Roman household codes that existed at the time—but he's changing them in a significant way. You see, the Roman household codes had submission instructions only for women and children. The men could do whatever they wanted, because Romans believed women and children were ontologically inferior.

Here is how a second-century Roman lawyer named Gaius describes the state of affairs in his famous work *Institutes*:

> The public law of Rome did not recognize women at all. Women were answerable for their misdeeds to the family judge, the father or husband. . . . Men were punished by the state, but the women had to be given over to the private jurisdiction of the family. It should be noted that nothing can be granted in the way of justice to those under power; i.e., to slaves, children and wives. For it is reasonable to conclude that, since these persons can own no property, they are incompetent to claim anything in point of law.[5]

Slaves, children, and women were unable to make any legal claim; they were the property of the husband or father. And this patriarch was given free rein to be judge, jury, even executioner. We have documented evidence of husbands legally executing their wives for everything from infidelity to drinking wine without permission.[6]

Now, Gaius didn't come up with these categories. These were long-standing household divisions in Greco-Roman culture dating back to Socrates, Plato, Aristotle, and beyond. In fact, many biblical scholars believe that Paul borrowed much of his language from published copies of these secular household codes. Here is Aristotle's version:

> In a complete household there are three relations: 1) that of the master to the slave; 2) of the husband to the wife; 3) of the parent to the child. What is and ought to be the character of each of these? The master rules over the slave despotically, the husband over the wife constitutionally, but in neither case do they take turns of ruling and being ruled after the manner of constitutional states, because the difference between them is permanent.

5. Gaius, *Institutes of Gaius*, trans. W. M. Gordon and O. F. Robinson (Duckworth, 1988), 80–81.

6. Fragment of "De dote," in Marcus Porcius Cato, *M. Catonis praeter librum de re rustica quae extant*, ed. H. Jordan (Leipzig, 1860), 68.

> The rule of the father or elder over the child is like that of the king over his subjects.[7]

The master rules over the slave with absolute power, often exercised in a cruel way. The husband rules over the wife constitutionally, which means in a way that accords with the natural laws of order. The father rules over the child like a king over his subjects. There is no taking turns in this rulership because the difference between the parties is permanent. It is the nature of things, Aristotle says.

Paul disagrees. In light of the gospel of Jesus Christ and the new community Jesus has established based on the mutuality and flourishing of all people, Paul believes men need to be submissive too. In fact, Paul says men should be willing to lay down their lives for women and children.

Jesus and Paul Were Feminists

If we use a common definition of a "feminist"—"one who believes in, and is committed to, the idea of true equality between the sexes, and that means the development of women to their fullest potential and full partnership, and participation by women in all decisions of society"[8]—then we can easily argue that Paul was one of the world's first feminists.

In Ephesians 5 and throughout his other letters, Paul teaches mutual submission between the sexes and equality for women. So not only do biblical women contradict female subjugation, but the New Testament also subverts the patriarchal systems prevalent in the first century by encouraging a gender ethic

7. Aristotle, *Politics* 1.12, trans. H. Rackham (Harvard University Press, 1932), 67.

8. Betty Friedan, quoted in "A Feminist? Definition Varies with the Woman," *New York Times*, November 8, 1975, https://www.nytimes.com/1975/11/08/archives/a-feminist-definition-varies-with-the-woman.html.

based on full equality in Christ. Why does Paul do this? Because it's what Jesus did. I'm fairly active on Twitter[9] and have seen a lot of great tweets over the years, but this one, from nonprofit leader Carlos Rodríguez, is one of my favorites:

> Jesus protected women.
> Empowered women.
> Honored women publicly.
> Released the voice of women.
> Confided in women.
> Was funded by women.
> Celebrated women by name.
> Learned from women.
> Respected women.
> And spoke of women as examples to follow.[10]

Those are not just random phrases Carlos threw together. They are facts based on biblical stories of Jesus interacting with women.

- He protected women like the one about to be stoned in John 8.
- He empowered women like the bleeding woman in Mark 5.
- He honored women publicly like the woman who anointed him in Matthew 26.
- He released the voice of women like the Samaritan woman at the well in John 4.
- He confided in women like Martha in John 11.

9. I refuse to call it X.

10. Carlos A. Rodríguez (@CarlosHappyNPO), "Dear Church," Twitter (now X), February 10, 2018, https://x.com/CarlosHappyNPO/status/962382920341213184.

- He was funded by women like Joanna and Susanna in Luke 8.
- He celebrated women by name like his disciple Mary in Luke 10.
- He learned from women like the Canaanite woman in Matthew 15.
- He respected women like the woman he called "daughter of Abraham" in Luke 13.
- And he spoke of women as examples to follow, like Mary Magdalene, who would go on to be a key leader in the early church and today is known as the apostle to the apostles.

Throughout Scripture, there are examples of women teaching, preaching, and pastoring. The biblical authors repeatedly call all these things "spiritual gifts," which means they are empowered by the Spirit of God. We are vessels for God to express these gifts, so why would the gender of the vessel be a hindrance to God? How small would our God have to be if he were unable or unwilling to empower women through the Holy Spirit?

Years ago, I was at a pastors' conference when a guy walked up to me and angrily said, "I can't believe you allow women to pastor and preach at your church."

"I don't," I replied.

He looked confused for a second and then said, "Oh, good. I heard they were."

I responded, "Oh no, you heard right. Women have preached and pastored at our church since day one. It's just not me who 'allows' it. Jesus does. All I do is get out of the way and cheer them on."

Growing up, I was told that God could only work through the pastoring and preaching of men, but I've come to know that is simply wrong. I know it because of the examples of women throughout Scripture and because of the incredible women who have led, taught, and mentored me over the years. I also know it because of so many women I've had the privilege to lead alongside and learn from at our church.

Women and men living and leading as equals is the way of Jesus, but somewhere along the way, Christians allowed the patriarchal norms of society to influence how we treat women. We allowed misogynistic men to distort the teachings of Jesus and the early church. And we allowed a handful of descriptive Bible verses to be plucked out of context and used to subjugate women.

For far too long in the church, sexism has been baptized and called God's will. Enough is enough. Even within deeply patriarchal cultures, we see Jesus and the early church elevating and empowering women.

Depending on what you've been taught about women's roles in church, you might be wondering if you've been lied to. I believe you have. Now, you may have been lied to by incredibly well-meaning people who were also lied to and told this is God's will for women. The goal is not to tear down every leader or church that is getting this wrong. The goal is to build something new modeled after something very old—that very first all-inclusive church. The goal is to tell the truth about God's will for women and create spaces where people of any gender, age, race, socioeconomic status, sexual orientation, background, and ability can experience freedom and the fullness of life that Jesus desires for them.

And we get to do this vital work not in spite of Scripture but undergirded by it. When we read the Bible through the context lens, it's easy to see that this was God's will for us all along.

9

the flourishing lens

"I Have Come That They May Have Life Abundantly"

> There can be no love without justice.
>
> —bell hooks, *All About Love*

Years ago, a woman named Samantha asked if we could get coffee so she could talk about something that was troubling her. I agreed and we picked a date. A few days later, she sat down across from me with a cup of coffee in her hand and a distressed look on her face.

It's important to know that Samantha was new to Christianity. She'd been exposed to the church as a child but had left after suffering significant abuse and spiritual trauma. Once, she told me, she had witnessed a deacon escort a Black family out of her childhood church because the pastor believed "race mixing" was forbidden in the Bible.

All throughout her adolescence and adulthood, Samantha stayed as far away from Christians as possible, but she ended up coming back to faith at our church. The only Christians she'd maintained relationships with during those years were her grandparents. They were lifelong churchgoers, and Samantha would attend with them whenever she visited.

But on her last visit, something concerning happened. When Samantha arrived at their home, the power was out and the house was freezing. There hadn't been any recent storms, so she asked her grandparents why the electricity wasn't working. They told her they couldn't pay the bill and that it had been turned off a few days before. She also noticed they had very little food in the home.

Samantha told me her grandparents had been on a fixed income for years and had budgeted to have enough money to cover their basic needs, so it was strange that they suddenly didn't have money to pay bills or buy groceries. Something didn't add up. She asked them what had happened.

"Our church said everyone needed to increase their giving," they told her.

Samantha was incredulous. "What? So you increased your giving so much that you can't buy food or pay for electricity?"

"Yes. Our pastor said giving everything we have to God demonstrates our faithfulness, just like the widow who was praised by Jesus for giving her last two coins."

Samantha looked at me as angry tears gathered in the corners of her eyes. She was outraged. Then she asked me if I had heard the story of the widow. She wanted to know if that's how Christians really ought to give to the church.

I knew the story. Every time I'd heard it preached, the application was the same: This woman gave all she had to God, and we should too. But during our meeting, I realized I'd never met anyone who'd actually done it. I'd never heard of people who went without groceries or electricity because they gave all their money to the church, even though it's the logical conclusion of that interpretation.

I sat there, trying to think of answers to this woman's questions, and I knew we'd messed up. I knew there was absolutely nothing pleasing to Christ about an elderly couple without food and power. I knew that Jesus said he came to preach good news for the poor and freedom for the oppressed, not to multiply poverty and make vulnerable people even more vulnerable.

Something I had been taught to believe was coming into conflict with something I experienced. I was taught to believe that God wants all of us to give everything we have, just like the widow, but when I experienced the logical end of that belief—my friend's grandparents suffering—I knew it couldn't be right.

Flourishing and Liberation Theology

From the opening words of the Bible to the final ones, God has a consistent desire for all of creation: flourishing. Flourishing is what defines the garden of Eden in Genesis and the new heaven and new earth in Revelation—the two clearest pictures of God's design for this world.

Flourishing for all people is also what defines God's kingdom, which is the thing Jesus spent the majority of his preaching ministry talking about. In John 10:10, Jesus gives us a brief picture of why he came to earth: "I have come that they may have life, and have it to the full."

But things get in the way of flourishing. We hurt ourselves, we hurt others, we build systems that oppress people, and we don't take care of the creation that God has entrusted to us. So there is a wide gap between what we experience and what God wants us to experience. The bridge over that chasm is liberation—freedom from anything and everything that prevents flourishing. And once we know to look for it, we see that liberation is all over Scripture.

Theologian James Cone says bluntly, "Any theology that is indifferent to the theme of liberation is not Christian theology. . . . I didn't need a doctorate in theology to know that liberation defined the heart of Jesus's ministry."[1]

So what is liberation theology?

Brothers Leonardo and Clodovis Boff, Catholic theologians and philosophers, define liberation theology as the "commitment to the life, cause, and struggle of these millions of debased and marginalized human beings [the poor and the oppressed], a commitment to ending this historical-social iniquity."[2]

In 1968, Father Pedro Arrupe coined the phrase "God's preferential option for the poor" in a letter to Jesuits, a Catholic order of priests, in Latin America. This idea that God chooses to exhibit extraordinary care for people on the margins became a cornerstone of liberation theology.

Although God certainly loves all of humanity equally, Scripture shows us time and time again that God pays unique attention to the poor and the oppressed. This makes perfect sense when you think about it. If God truly is the loving parent of all people, then God would naturally show special concern for the children who are suffering most. More than two thousand Bible verses testify to God's special concern for marginalized people. Even though the good news about Jesus is for everyone, it first

1. James Cone, "The Relationship of the Christian Faith to Political Praxis," lecture, Princeton Theological Seminary, Princeton, NJ, March 12, 1980.

2. Leonardo Boff and Clodovis Boff, *Introducing Liberation Theology* (Orbis Books, 1987), 2.

came to those on the margins of society: fishermen, farmers, shepherds, and a teenage girl.

Jesus even kicks off his public ministry by preaching this message. He stands up in his childhood synagogue and reads from the prophet Isaiah, saying, “The Spirit of the Lord is on me, because he has anointed me to proclaim good news to the poor. He has sent me to proclaim freedom for the prisoners and recovery of sight for the blind, to set the oppressed free, to proclaim the year of the Lord’s favor” (Luke 4:18–19).

In Jesus’s most famous teaching, the Sermon on the Mount, he makes the same points again, but this special concern for the marginalized is most clearly articulated in Jesus’s words found in Matthew 25: “Truly I tell you, whatever you did for one of the least of these brothers and sisters of mine, you did for me. . . . Truly I tell you, whatever you did not do for one of the least of these, you did not do for me” (25:40, 45).

Jesus says we will be judged by God for how we meet the needs of poor and oppressed people, because how we treat them is how we treat Jesus. Even though the concept of liberation theology wasn’t fully formed until the 1960s, its roots stretch back much further. Referencing Matthew 25, Augustine of Hippo in his fourth-century preaching articulated Jesus’s oneness with the poor: “Christ is needy when a poor person is in need. . . . Christ is hungry when poor people are hungry.”[3]

Jesus is on the side of liberation for the poor, the suffering, and the downtrodden. If we are on that side, he is there with us. If we are not, he beckons us to join him there. If we are reading the Bible in ways that lead to oppression rather than liberation, we are sabotaging the work of God and subverting the message of Christ.

3. Augustine, Sermon 38 and Sermon 390, quoted in “The Poor,” AUGNET, accessed March 4, 2025, http://www.augnet.org/en/works-of-augustine/his-ideas/2325-the-poor.

Let me put the point even more directly: If the version of Christianity we are proclaiming does not prioritize liberation for the marginalized, then it is not the Christianity of Jesus Christ.

Robert Chao Romero, a pastor, immigration lawyer, and professor at UCLA, expounds on Jesus's commitment to liberation in his book *Brown Church*: "Jesus clearly articulates a preferential option for immigrants, the poor, and all who are disregarded by society. Jesus takes their side. Not only that, but he identifies so closely with the struggles of the poor that he sees himself in them. If we love him, then we will love the poor. When we love the poor, we are loving him. According to Jesus, our compassion towards the most vulnerable of society is a barometer of the sincerity of our relationship with him."[4]

Pastor and womanist theologian[5] Karen Mosby-Avery is even more candid: "We cannot continue to bear the name Christian . . . if we will not join God in eliminating marginalized people's suffering, if we will not join Christ in rebelling against injustice."[6]

Liberation theology teaches us how to bridge the gap between the flourishing God desires for all humans and the brokenness many of us are experiencing every day. We live in a broken world. No human is exempt from the problems and pain that

4. Robert Chao Romero, *Brown Church: Five Centuries of Latina/o Social Justice, Theology, and Identity* (IVP Academic, 2020), 148–49.

5. Womanist theology is a field of study and religious thought that emerged in the 1980s, building on the concept of womanism introduced by Alice Walker in her book *In Search of Our Mothers' Gardens: Womanist Prose* (Harcourt, 1983). It focuses on the religious experiences, thoughts, and practices of Black women, specifically addressing the intersections of race, gender, and class. It emerged as a response to the limitations of both feminist theology (which often centered on White women's experiences) and Black liberation theology (which tended to prioritize male perspectives). Womanist theologians like Delores S. Williams, Wilda Gafney, Renita Weems, Love Sechrest, Kelly Brown Douglas, Jacquelyn Grant, and many others are doing incredible work in this area, and I highly recommend them.

6. Karen E. Mosby-Avery, "Black Theology and the Black Church," in *Living Stones in the Household of God: The Legacy and Future of Black Theology*, ed. Linda E. Thomas (Fortress, 2004), 35.

accompany us on this journey through life. We have all been hurt, and we have all hurt others.

But I want to clarify something about this universal pain and brokenness: Our world wasn't broken by mistake. Many times we picture the world like a snow globe that was accidentally dropped and shattered into a million little pieces, but that's not what Scripture tells us. The biblical authors make it clear that God's perfect world was broken when we humans decided to turn our backs on God's way and go our own way. In other words, the world was broken by intentional choices. And most of those choices involved an individual or group exerting power over another individual or group—usually through violence and exploitation.

Choices involving domination are still being made today. We see them all around us, in our neighborhoods and in countries on the other side of the globe. We also continue to navigate the brokenness caused by individual and collective choices made by people who came before us.

Our world is home to massive inequalities because of people exerting power over others. Our world is broken in a way that pits God's image bearers against one another and rewards oppression for the purpose of domination. Mark Labberton, president emeritus of Fuller Theological Seminary, puts it like this: "Each of us participates in a world of disordered power, personal and systemic. It's everywhere, and none of us are free from being its perpetrators or victims—and frequently we are both."[7]

No one is exempt from this broken world of disordered power. And as Labberton says so well, most of us receive both advantages and disadvantages from it. We are both perpetrators and victims, privileged and oppressed.

7. Mark Labberton, foreword to *Subversive Witness: Scripture's Call to Leverage Privilege*, by Dominique DuBois Gilliard (Zondervan Reflective, 2021), xv.

Most of us avoid talking about these topics because doing so can make us feel uncomfortable and vulnerable. This is especially true for those of us who experience more privilege and advantage. However, understanding the brokenness of our world, the disordered power that exists inside it, and how people experience both privilege and oppression is vital if we want to participate in Jesus-centered liberation work and read Scripture in a way that produces flourishing rather than pain.

Liberation is not haphazardly trying to pick up the broken pieces of our world and put them back together. Liberation is choosing to confront the disordered power. It is standing up to those who try to dominate others and standing up for the marginalized. It is putting Scripture into practice in ways that lift people up rather than tear them down.

God of Justice

Scripture often calls this work "justice," and we are told by the prophet Isaiah that "the Lord is a God of justice" (Isa. 30:18). But we are living in a cultural moment when justice and liberation are under attack, especially by people who claim the name of Christ.

Turn on Christian TV, follow some famous Christians on social media, or listen to clips from prominent pastors, and it won't be long before you hear justice being decried. People use terms like "social justice warrior" and "woke" pejoratively. They claim that critical race theory and DEI (diversity, equity, and inclusion) are a threat to the church. They say things like "don't get political" or "just preach the gospel." They do all of this in an attempt to shame people into not pursuing justice.

It probably comes as no surprise to you that most of the folks attacking justice share not only my Christian faith but also my skin color. As my friend Jemar Tisby says, "Many white

Christians have become de facto defenders of an unjust status quo by maintaining that Christians should not get involved in matters of public justice."[8]

Years ago, I would have said this anti-liberation posture made no sense to me. Why would anyone be against helping people who are hurting? But after spending the last few years learning from and being led by Christians of color who have been a part of liberation movements for decades, I've come to understand this is all purposeful.

If someone receives money, power, or political gain from injustice, then demonizing justice is the most effective way to ensure the perpetuation of those benefits. That's why it's such a red flag when people say it's "divisive" to talk about racism, sexism, nationalism, homophobia, ableism, or any other form of oppression. Justice is divisive only to those benefiting from injustice. Or to put it more bluntly, the only people standing against liberation are the ones who benefit from oppression.

There is a popular but tired refrain among Christians that pursuing liberation is unbiblical and that we should just stick to "preaching the gospel." But what is the gospel reduced to if it does not include justice? A get out of hell free card? A collection of culturally influenced morals? A set of beliefs we assent to with our minds that never permeate our hearts? What part of life should the gospel not affect? Shouldn't the good news of Jesus Christ change everything? Shouldn't the Scriptures inform how we live every part of our lives?

If the gospel does not include liberation for all people, then it is not the gospel of Jesus Christ. If the gospel does not bring good news to both the spiritually and the socially broken, then it is not the good news that Jesus preached.

8. Jemar Tisby, *How to Fight Racism: Courageous Christianity and the Journey Toward Racial Justice* (Zondervan Reflective, 2021), 142.

When it comes to the work of Jesus, social liberation and spiritual liberation are never in opposition to each other. Any gospel work should be committed to holistic justice, concerned with the flourishing of people's souls and bodies.

I wholeheartedly agree with Martin Luther King Jr., who says, "There are some who still find the cross a stumbling block, and others consider it foolishness, but I am more convinced than ever before that it is the power of God unto social and individual salvation."[9]

Calling liberation "unbiblical" is one of the most unbiblical statements one can make. From Genesis to Revelation, God pursues liberation for the marginalized and calls us to join in on that same work. This has been the legacy of God's people since the beginning, and it continues to be our calling today.

We are not only called to read the Bible in ways that lead to liberation and flourishing but also commanded to put liberation into action by pushing back against injustice, oppression, and marginalization of all kinds. Throughout both the Old Testament and the New Testament, from Moses to Mary, we see God's people doing the work of liberation. And our God of justice is still using people to accomplish the same work today. If you're wondering what that might look like, Mitsuye Endo and James Purcell give us a great example.

Liberation from Internment Camps

On February 19, 1942, President Franklin Roosevelt signed executive order 9066, which authorized the incarceration of nearly 120,000 Japanese Americans during World War II, two-thirds of whom were born and raised in the United States. Tens of

9. Martin Luther King Jr., "Suffering and Faith," *Christian Century*, April 27, 1960, 510, available at https://kinginstitute.stanford.edu/king-papers/documents/suffering-and-faith.

thousands of Americans were taken from their homes, stripped of their property, businesses, and savings, and forced to live in internment camps. Many of the camps had been horse-racing tracks where the living quarters were converted livestock stalls. For almost three years, Japanese Americans lived in those horrifying conditions. Until God used the courageous work of Mitsuye Endo and James Purcell to help bring liberation.

Endo was a Japanese American citizen, born in Sacramento in 1920. She grew up in the Methodist church and got a clerical job after high school. Endo was twenty-two years old when she and her family were rounded up and taken to the Tule Lake internment camp in a remote part of California. They remained there for years, even as Endo's older brother fought in the US Army's 442nd Regiment.

Purcell was a White guy born in San Francisco in 1906. When executive order 9066 came down, he went to work for the Japanese American Citizens League (JACL) as a lawyer, advocating on behalf of incarcerated Japanese Americans. Purcell and the JACL needed a primary plaintiff to challenge the incarceration. They sent word to Endo to see if she was willing to be the primary plaintiff in the case. Endo was hesitant but decided to say yes. Years later, she told an author, "It was awfully hard for me. I agreed to do it at that moment, because they said it's for the good of everybody, and so I said, well if that's it, I'll go ahead and do it."[10]

Purcell and Endo filed their petition on July 12, 1942, beginning a chain of events that eventually led to the US Supreme Court ruling in her favor in December 1944, initiating the release of all Japanese Americans from incarceration and the end of internment camps. Endo stayed incarcerated the entire time the

10. John Tateishi, *And Justice for All: An Oral History of the Japanese American Detention Camps* (University of Washington Press, 1999), 61.

courts debated her case. At one point, the government offered to let her return home in exchange for dropping the lawsuit. She refused.

Although you and I may never find ourselves in an internment camp, like Endo did, or arguing a case before the Supreme Court, like Purcell did, our calling from God is the same as theirs—to fight for liberation on behalf of everyone. This becomes even more important at a time when many perceive Christians as perpetrators of injustice rather than pursuers of justice.

As the Boff brothers write, "Commitment to the liberation of the millions of the oppressed of our world restores to the gospel the credibility it had at the beginning and at the great periods of holiness and prophetic witness in history."[11]

Choosing to put on the flourishing lens when reading Scripture means choosing interpretations that lead to liberation and flourishing for all people, especially the most vulnerable and those on the margins.

Flourishing for a Widow

What does interpreting the story of the widow's mite look like through the flourishing lens? The story begins in chapter 21 of Luke's account of Jesus's life: "As Jesus looked up, he saw the rich putting their gifts into the temple treasury. He also saw a poor widow put in two very small copper coins. 'Truly I tell you,' he said, 'this poor widow has put in more than all the others. All these people gave their gifts out of their wealth; but she out of her poverty put in all she had to live on'" (Luke 21:1–4).

The rich people give a small percentage of their wealth, but the widow gives everything she has. Again, many church leaders have interpreted the story to mean that hearers should be like

11. Boff and Boff, *Introducing Liberation Theology*, 9.

the widow and give everything they have too. But that teaching is nowhere to be found in these verses. Jesus doesn't say a single positive thing about the widow's donation. Jesus doesn't say, "She gave all she had, and you should too." He doesn't point out her tithe and then say, "Go and do likewise," as he does in other places. Jesus describes the widow's gift without commentary and then starts talking about something else.

So why does Jesus mention it? Why doesn't he explain himself more fully? Because these verses are not the beginning of a section but the end of one.

The passage we just read starts in verse 1 of chapter 21, but chapters and verses weren't added to Scripture until the sixteenth century, about fifteen hundred years after Luke wrote his Gospel. So it might seem like Luke 21:1 is the start of a new teaching, but in fact, it's a continuation of Luke 20, where Jesus is teaching in the temple courts.

Let me show you the verses right before the widow comes on the scene, and let's see if they help illuminate a better reading of this passage:

> While all the people were listening, Jesus said to his disciples, "Beware of the teachers of the law. They like to walk around in flowing robes and love to be greeted with respect in the marketplaces and have the most important seats in the synagogues and the places of honor at banquets. They devour widows' houses and for a show make lengthy prayers. These men will be punished most severely."
>
> As Jesus looked up, he saw the rich putting their gifts into the temple treasury. He also saw a poor widow put in two very small copper coins. "Truly I tell you," he said, "this poor widow has put in more than all the others. All these people gave their gifts out of their wealth; but she out of her poverty put in all she had to live on." (Luke 20:45–21:4)

While teaching in the temple, Jesus warns the people gathered around him about a group of leaders who care more about their power and wealth than the lives of downtrodden, marginalized people. He calls out teachers of the law who "devour widows' houses" and promises that they will be punished.

We don't know the exact means by which these corrupt men "devour widows' houses,"[12] but we do know that when a woman's husband died in that culture, the widow was almost always left with two things: debt and an inability to make money. Evidently, some teachers of the law were exploiting widows' vulnerable position to siphon off what little resources they had left.

It's important to note that this isn't a condemnation of Judaism or Jewish leaders at large. After all, Jesus was both Jewish and a leader in the Jewish community. As Lamar Williamson says, "Jesus does not attack Judaism or Jewish religious practices. The crowd that 'heard him gladly' (v. 37) consisted of Jews who had come to the Temple to fulfill religious obligations that Jesus himself acknowledged. What Jesus does attack is egotism and avarice masked in the vestments of religious learning and practices."[13]

Jesus is attacking exploitation rationalized by religion and protected by empire. The oppressive rulers of the Roman Empire partnered with leaders like the priestly aristocracy in order to maintain order and collect taxes. These leaders were not only

12. Here are some possibilities: "Jesus pictures destruction when he speaks of the scribes 'devouring' the houses of the widows. They take from the group most in need and leave them devastated. The nature of the crime is not detailed, but four possibilities are suggested: (1) the temple authorities managed the property of widows dedicated to the temple in a way that took advantage of them, (2) the scribes took advantage of widows' hospitality, (3) the scribes took homes as pledges of debts they know could not be paid, or (4) they took fees for legal advice against the provision of the law." Darrell L. Bock, *Luke*, 2 vols., Baker Exegetical Commentary on the New Testament (Baker Academic, 1994–96), 2:2052.

13. Lamar Williamson Jr., *Mark*, Interpretation: A Bible Commentary for Teaching and Preaching (Westminster John Knox, 2009), 233.

abusing their power to exploit the vulnerable for personal gain but also doing so in alignment with their people's oppressors. All of this was in violation of Jewish law. God put special regulations in place to make sure widows and other vulnerable populations were taken care of: "At the end of every three years, bring all the tithes of that year's produce and store it in your towns, so that the Levites (who have no allotment or inheritance of their own) and the foreigners, the fatherless and the widows who live in your towns may come and eat and be satisfied, and so that the LORD your God may bless you in all the work of your hands" (Deut. 14:28–29).

What is described here is a practice many modern church leaders call tithing.[14] The purpose of this tithe was to take care of vulnerable people. But fast-forward to the time of Jesus, and we see these leaders perverting the purpose of tithing, pressuring the most vulnerable to give all they have so there is more money for themselves and for the Roman Empire. Again, this is explicitly forbidden by God: "Cursed is anyone who withholds justice from the foreigner, the fatherless or the widow" (Deut. 27:19).

Withholding justice makes Jesus angry—like flipping-tables angry. In fact, Jesus's condemnation of these exploitative practices is directly connected to him clearing out the temple, which happened just one day before. Here's the story:

> Jesus entered the temple courts and began driving out those who were buying and selling there. He overturned the tables of the money changers and the benches of those selling doves, and would not allow anyone to carry merchandise through the temple courts. And as he taught them, he said, "Is it not written: 'My house will be called a house of prayer for all nations'? But you have made it 'a den of robbers.'" (Mark 11:15–17)

14. A tithe is generally considered to be donating 10 percent of one's income.

As Jesus so eloquently puts it, these men have transformed a house of prayer into a den of robbers. They have corrupted a system meant to support the vulnerable by using it to exploit them instead. So Jesus flips over the money changers' tables and the benches of people selling doves and then drives all the people profiting from this oppression out of the temple courtyard.

He returns to the temple courts the next day to teach people a better way—the way God has always intended tithing to be practiced and generosity to be expressed. The way of liberation and flourishing for all people. When we take another look at this story through the flourishing lens, we clearly see that Jesus is not complimenting the widow's donation; Jesus is condemning the leaders' exploitation. Old Testament scholar Young-Sam Won puts it like this: "Jesus is not praising this widow. He's indicting the wickedness of the leaders and systems of the day. If the people tithed as God instructed and the temple stores were full, she would have been cared for as one of the vulnerable."[15]

These leaders claimed piety and demanded honor, yet they were partnering with the oppressive Roman Empire and lining their own pockets by stealing from the most vulnerable. They preyed on the people they were supposed to be caring for. Yet, to this day, some religious leaders use this story to do the exact same thing, including the pastor of Samantha's grandparents.

If tithing were being properly practiced, this widow would have been *receiving* money rather than giving it. If tithing were being properly practiced, Samantha's grandparents would have had electricity and all the food they could eat through the generosity of their church. Looking at this story through the flourishing lens not only allows us to interpret it in a more Christlike way but also equips us to better care for folks in need.

15. Sam Won (@SamObiWon), "Inspired by a recent Twitter conversation, let me connect some dots," Twitter (now X), September 18, 2022, https://x.com/SamObiWon/status/1571594187497160705.

This demonstrates the vital importance of choosing to take off harmful lenses and put on healthy ones. I appreciate what Episcopal priest Bryan Owen says:

> The story of the poor widow giving away everything she had to live on to the temple is a tragic reminder that religion can be used for evil and oppressive purposes. We live in a world filled with poverty, abuse, oppression, and exploitation. And we live in a world in which our Christian faith sometimes gets used to do the very things to others that break our Lord's heart. And yet, we know that the very same faith that can be twisted and manipulated to pilfer poor widows can also be used to feed the hungry, build houses for the homeless, care for the sick, befriend the lonely, and extend a hand of fellowship to those the world writes off as worthless.[16]

Even though Christianity in general (and the story of this widow specifically) has been weaponized to hurt people, this is not the only option. A better way of reading the Bible is through the flourishing lens, which yields an interpretation that helps uplift the oppressed, care for the marginalized, and promote liberation for all people.

I love this quote from Fannie Lou Hamer, a sharecropper turned activist during the civil rights movement of the 1960s: "Nobody's free until everybody's free."[17] We are in this together. My flourishing is tied up with yours and vice versa. The idea that nobody's free until everybody's free involves you, dear reader. Step into freedom. Step into the liberation offered through Jesus and his unconditional love. Leave behind the harmful lenses that hurt you and your neighbors, and put on the flourishing lens, which leads to fullness of life for absolutely everyone.

16. Bryan Owen, "Rescuing the Poor Widow," *Covenant*, Living Church, September 24, 2021, https://covenant.livingchurch.org/2021/09/24/rescuing-the-poor-widow.

17. Fannie Lou Hamer, *The Speeches of Fannie Lou Hamer: To Tell It Like It Is*, ed. Maegan Parker Brooks and Davis W. Houck (University Press of Mississippi, 2010), 139.

10

the fruitfulness lens

"By Their Fruit You Will Recognize Them"

> For love is not what we do after we get the other things done, if we have any energy left over. Love is what we do, period. It is not how we work; it is our work.
>
> —Eugene Peterson, *This Hallelujah Banquet*

In my seminary days, I enrolled in a church-planting class, intrigued by the idea of starting a new church. The district superintendent of the Evangelical Free Church of America (EFCA) overseeing Texas and Oklahoma frequented my class to recruit potential church planters, and we met one day after the lecture ended. A few days later, over a cafeteria lunch, I shared the vision of Restore and what my wife and I believed God was calling us to do.

Our discussion broached some contentious topics. I told him we were committed to being fully inclusive, meaning that regardless of someone's age, race, gender, disability, socioeconomic status, or sexual orientation, they could fully participate in every part of our church. He looked a little confused. "So gay people can be members and leaders?" he asked.

"Yes," I said. "LGBTQ+ folks won't have any restrictions based on their sexual orientation, gender, or relationship status. They can serve, lead, take communion, get married, and anything else the church offers. Because we know this isn't our church; it's Jesus's church. And we know it's not our table; it's Jesus's table. He decides who gets to sit with him, and he's been incredibly clear—whoever wants a seat has one."

The superintendent told me that Restore would likely be the only church in the district with a posture like that but that there were no policies forbidding it. The denomination identifies as a big-tent movement, rooted in creedal Christian doctrines (evangelical) and committed to local church autonomy (free) in everything else.

As a somewhat naive twenty-five-year-old, I loved the idea of a big-tent movement, so we decided to join forces with them. I went through the EFCA's leadership training program and began fostering deep connections with other pastors in the denomination.

Not long after Restore opened in February 2016, we celebrated our first annual Bapticue. Bapticue (a word we coined by combining "baptisms" and "BBQ"[1]) is a church picnic of sorts with a BBQ lunch, bounce houses, games, and baptisms.

Our first year, we baptized ten folks, including a woman named Shayna. Her childhood was marked by substantial church trauma that left scars deep enough to foster anger toward both God and Christianity.

1. Texas BBQ, especially brisket, is absolutely superior to anything else calling itself BBQ in the world.

When Shayna and I first met for coffee, she made it clear that she harbored doubts about Restore specifically and Christianity more broadly. I think the first words out of her mouth were "Just so you know, I don't believe any of this stuff." Despite this, a friendship blossomed, and a few months later, she decided to follow Jesus after experiencing the radical love of God at Restore. Shayna is still a close friend, and baptizing her that day at Bapticue is one of the highlights of my ministry life.

Shayna is also a lesbian. I honestly didn't think much about her sexual orientation during the baptism or even when Shayna and her wife dedicated their three children at our first Kid Dedication[2] a few weeks later. They were just normal church members like anyone else. But a group of EFCA pastors found out and got angry. Initially, they approached the district superintendent, who let them know we hadn't actually broken any rules. The Texas-Oklahoma district had no policies concerning LGBTQ+ inclusion.

But the pastors were persistent, so the superintendent told them to contact the national office with their complaint, and they did. This triggered an extensive investigation of Restore, requiring me to testify multiple times before a disciplinary board. When push came to shove, there were no grounds to kick us out of the denomination, but the national office pressured the district to change its bylaws and adopt a policy limiting the involvement of LGBTQ+ folks in congregations. It took the better part of two years, but the district finally passed the anti-LGBTQ+ policy. I still remember the final disciplinary hearing. At the conclusion of the meeting, they asked if I had any final words to share. I said, "I just want us all to take a moment and sit with

2. A time when parents bring their kids before God and our church family to ask for grace, wisdom, and support as they carry out the great responsibility of raising children.

the fact that y'all are kicking our church out of this denomination because a woman who happens to be a lesbian had a radical encounter with the love of Jesus at Restore, placed her faith in Christ, and I baptized her."

After a long silence, the board chairman said, "We'll be in touch." A few days later, we were officially kicked out of the denomination. They also stripped me of my ministry license and threatened legal action against us. The hardest part wasn't the denominational fallout, though. The most profound pain came from having pastors I'd assumed would be friends for life cut me off or worse. One man, who just a couple of years before had stood with me in the hospital room and prayed over my son who was suffering from seizures, told me I was leading my family and our church down a path to damnation.

This is not the only time something like this has happened at Restore because of our commitment to inclusion. We've been removed from church networks; we've lost tens of thousands of dollars in funding; and I've been told I'm going to hell more times than I can count.

Honestly, though, none of that comes close to the goodness our community has experienced as a result of LGBTQ+ folks fully participating and leading at Restore. The conversations, messages, hugs, and tears I've been able to share with people from the queer community make all the challenges worth it.

I also know that what we've been through is nothing compared to what LGBTQ+ folks have been through. Members of the queer community have been called "abominations," disowned by their families, condemned to hell, and even tortured and abused through conversion therapy—all at the hands of Christians. These are not just statistics; they are stories. And they are the stories of people I love. People in this book. People I consider to be my closest friends.

- One of these friends was locked in a basement and repeatedly assaulted during her "Christian" conversion therapy as a teenager.
- Another friend was kicked out of church during his transition and the pastor told everyone in the congregation to treat him like he was dead until he repented.
- One of my friends from childhood came out to her parents, and the first words out of her dad's mouth were "You've ruined our family and brought the wrath of God upon us."
- After coming out, another friend's son was completely shunned by the other students at his church. They literally refused to speak to him when he would attend youth group meetings.

But do you know what I find most incredible about my friends and so many other queer Christians? Through it all, they didn't give up on Jesus. The unrelenting faith of LGBTQ+ Christians astounds and inspires me.

Recently, I met a gay man who has been pastoring for over twenty-five years. He grew up in fundamentalist churches, was a student at Bob Jones University, and has faced intense homophobia throughout his life.

When I asked this pastor how he has persevered all these years, he said, "I'm not going to let anybody take Jesus from me."

You Will Know Them by Their Fruit

The final healthy lens we are going to look at is the fruitfulness lens, which comes from the words of Jesus: "Every good tree bears good fruit, but a bad tree bears bad fruit. . . . By their fruit you will recognize them" (Matt. 7:17, 20). Jesus asserts that the defining marker of his followers is the bearing of good fruit.

What is this good fruit? Scripture says, "The fruit of the Spirit is love, joy, peace, forbearance, kindness, goodness, faithfulness, gentleness and self-control" (Gal. 5:22–23). This means that if our biblical interpretation isn't producing more love, joy, peace, forbearance, kindness, goodness, faithfulness, gentleness, and self-control in us and through us, then our interpretation is not being led by the Spirit of Jesus. Let me be clear: If the way we read the Bible produces poisonous fruit rather than the fruit of the Spirit, we are reading it wrong.

I can think of few examples more insidious than the poisonous fruit produced by biblical interpretations weaponized against LGBTQ+ Christians to keep them out of the church and condemn their existence. I've already told you some stories to illustrate this truth, but let me give you some statistics and facts as well:

- Eighty-three percent of LGBTQ+ folks were raised in a Christian church.[3] That's higher than the national average of people raised in the church.
- At least once in their lives, 96 percent of LGBTQ+ folks have prayed for God to make them straight.[4]
- Many LGBTQ+ people tried or were forced to try orientation change through conversion therapy—a practice that is now illegal in twenty-six states and the District of Columbia. Why is it illegal? Because LGBTQ+ people who have gone through conversion therapy are more likely than those who haven't to use illicit drugs, twice as likely

3. Andrew Marin, *Us Versus Us: The Untold Story of Religion and the LGBT Community* (NavPress, 2016), 176.

4. Marin, *Us Versus Us*, 113.

to face depression, two and a half times more likely to die by suicide, and three times more likely to die by suicide if a religious leader encouraged them to undergo that treatment.[5] Four out of five people who underwent conversion therapy did so under the leadership of a religious leader rather than a licensed therapist, which means they were unprotected by legislation.[6]

- In 2019, the president of Exodus International—at one time, the leading conversion therapy organization worldwide—said, "No one changes their orientation; it doesn't happen. No therapy, no ministry, no prayer meeting, no nothing—you cannot change your sexual orientation."[7]
- A survey of LGBTQ+ young adults aged eighteen to twenty-four found that parents' negative religious beliefs about homosexuality were associated with a doubling of the risk of suicide attempts.[8]
- About 40 percent of America's 1.6 million homeless youth are LGBTQ+,[9] and many of them were kicked out of their homes due to their sexual orientation and/or gender identity. According to the Ali Forney Center (a New York–based homeless shelter serving LGBTQ+ youth), 90 percent of their clients were rejected due to

5. "The Need for Reform," Reformation Project, accessed December 16, 2024, https://reformationproject.org/the-need.

6. Williams Institute, UCLA School of Law, "LGB People Who Have Undergone Conversion Therapy Almost Twice as Likely to Attempt Suicide," press release, June 15, 2020, https://williamsinstitute.law.ucla.edu/press/lgb-suicide-ct-press-release.

7. "Need for Reform."

8. "Religiosity and Suicidality Among LGBTQ Youth," Trevor Project, April 14, 2020, https://www.thetrevorproject.org/research-briefs/religiosity-and-suicidality-among-lgbtq-youth.

9. "The Cost of Coming Out: LGBT Youth Homelessness," Lesley University, accessed December 16, 2024, https://lesley.edu/article/the-cost-of-coming-out-lgbt-youth-homelessness.

their parents' religious beliefs.[10] Twenty-eight percent of LGBTQ+ youths report experiencing homelessness or housing instability during their lives.[11]

- LGBTQ+ children who are rejected by their families are 8.4 times more likely to attempt suicide, 5.9 times more likely to have high levels of depression, and 3.4 times more likely to use illegal drugs than LGBTQ+ children who have supportive families.[12]
- In fact, having just one accepting adult reduces the risk of a suicide attempt among LGBTQ+ young people by 40 percent.[13]
- Considering how often anti-LGBTQ+ rhetoric and conversion therapy are undergirded by Christian beliefs, it's not surprising that 54 percent of LGBTQ+ folks leave their religious community after age eighteen. Twenty-seven percent of Americans leave faith communities as adults, which means that LGBTQ+ people are leaving the church at double the rate of everyone else.[14]

Here is my point: The way we interpret the biblical passages that seemingly address LGBTQ+ people is a matter of life and death. This isn't hyperbole. I have buried far too many queer people who spent their lives trying to find their place in the church, only to be met with conditional acceptance or outright

10. Carl Siciliano, "LGBTQ Teens Are Expelled from Their Homes by Religious Parents. We Must Do Better," Outreach, March 12, 2023, https://outreach.faith/2023/03/lgbtq-teens-are-expelled-from-their-homes-by-religious-parents-we-must-do-better.

11. "New Report Shows Homelessness, Housing Instability Linked to Increased Suicide Risk Among LGBTQ Youth," Trevor Project, February 3, 2022, https://www.thetrevorproject.org/blog/new-report-shows-homelessness-housing-instability-linked-to-increased-suicide-risk-among-lgbtq-youth.

12. "Religiosity and Suicidality Among LGBTQ Youth."

13. "Religiosity and Suicidality Among LGBTQ Youth."

14. Marin, *Us Versus Us*, 31.

rejection. I have counseled far too many LGBTQ+ folks who were told "Jesus loves you, but . . ." or "You're welcome here, but . . ." This is poisonous fruit. There should be absolutely no "buts" when it comes to the church loving and including LGBTQ+ folks.

We've witnessed a group of people completely leaving behind faith communities and the church missing out on the unique ways in which queer people bear God's image and express the fruit of the Spirit.

We need to get this right. Or more to the point, we have gotten it wrong for so long that we need to make it right. I believe any kind of discrimination based on sexual orientation or gender identity is wrong. I believe this not because it's cool or popular but because of what I see in Scripture. I believe the words and actions of both Jesus and the early church amount to a complete rejection of LGBTQ+ discrimination and a full embrace of sexual and gender minorities. Let me show you what I mean.

Jesus and Sexual/Gender Minorities

In Matthew 19, Jesus is asked a question about divorce. Some teachers of the law claimed divorce was permissible by the husband for any reason, and some said it was only for certain reasons. Remember, the issue is framed this way because, as we discussed in chapter 8, wives could not legally divorce their husbands in this culture. Jesus replies, "I tell you that anyone who divorces his wife, except for sexual immorality, and marries another woman commits adultery." The disciples then say to him, "If this is the situation between a husband and wife, it is better not to marry" (Matt. 19:9–10).

This response from the disciples is essentially "If I can't divorce my wife anytime and for any reason, then I don't even want to get married."

But as he often does, Jesus uses their response to make a bigger point. He says to them, "Not everyone can accept this word, but only those to whom it has been given. For there are eunuchs who were born that way, and there are eunuchs who have been made eunuchs by others—and there are those who choose to live like eunuchs for the sake of the kingdom of heaven. The one who can accept this should accept it" (Matt. 19:11–12).

Jesus mentions three kinds of people to whom his statement about divorce does not apply, using the word "eunuch" each time. So what is a eunuch? In the Bible, "eunuch" is an umbrella term used to describe someone we would now describe as being a sexual and/or gender minority.

Sometimes "eunuch" refers to people who have been castrated, either voluntarily or against their will. This happened for a variety of reasons. Sometimes people were castrated because of a job. Since people believed that eunuchs had no sex drive and were more trustworthy than non-eunuchs, they often castrated people who worked in finance or a house of royalty. Sometimes castration was done as punishment because a young boy didn't exhibit "masculine characteristics." And sometimes it was done voluntarily because of a disconnect the person felt with their sexuality or gender—a condition we now refer to as gender dysphoria. Other times in Scripture, "eunuch" refers more broadly to intersex people. And still other times, the term refers to people who choose to remain celibate for a variety of reasons.[15]

But the most important thing to understand about Jesus's words in Matthew 19 is that he's acknowledging people outside

15. For a deeper dive into eunuchs in the Bible, I recommend Megan K. DeFranza, *Sex Difference in Christian Theology: Male, Female, and Intersex in the Image of God* (Eerdmans, 2015); James V. Brownson, *Bible, Gender, and Sexuality: Reframing the Church's Debate on Same-Sex Relationships* (Eerdmans, 2013), chaps. 6, 7, 9, 11; Willie James Jennings, *Acts* (Westminster John Knox, 2017), 82–86; and F. P. Retief, J. F. G. Cilliers, and S. P. J. K. Riekert, "Eunuchs in the Bible," *Acta Theologica* 26, no. 2 (2006): 247–58, doi.org/10.4314/actat.v26i2.52578.

the sexual and gender norms of his time. To put it another way, Jesus is recognizing sexual and gender minorities without condemnation.

If you're reading this and you are a sexual or gender minority, a member of the LGBTQ+ community, this is beautiful proof that Jesus sees you. He talks about you in Scripture. And he includes you in his family.

Those listening to Jesus that day would have also been reminded of an Old Testament prophecy about eunuchs.

The Old Testament and Sexual/Gender Minorities

People who are considered sexual and gender minorities today were one of the most vulnerable populations in the ancient world. Because of this, Scripture says they cried out to God for help. Here is how God responds through the prophet Isaiah: "For this is what the Lord says: 'To the eunuchs who keep my Sabbaths, who choose what pleases me and hold fast to my covenant—to them I will give within my temple and its walls a memorial and a name better than sons and daughters; I will give them an everlasting name that will endure forever'" (Isa. 56:4–5).

Notice that God doesn't say he's going to fix or change these eunuchs. He simply says that if they follow him, he will welcome them into his home and his eternal family. If you're someone experiencing gender dysphoria or who identifies as nonbinary, I want you to grab hold of that promise. Even when you don't feel like you fit neatly into the category of "son" or "daughter," God promises to give you a name better than sons and daughters.

And the promise keeps going: "These I will bring to my holy mountain and give them joy in my house of prayer. Their burnt offerings and sacrifices will be accepted on my altar; for my house will be called a house of prayer for all nations" (Isa. 56:7).

I love that the passage ends by saying that God's house is "a house of prayer for all nations." That's the same phrase Jesus yells as he flips over tables in the temple courts just days before he is killed on the cross. The God of both the Old Testament and the New Testament, expressed most clearly in the person of Jesus Christ, declares that there is a room for anyone in his house and a seat for everyone at his table.

The Early Church and Sexual/Gender Minorities

For the early church, radical inclusion of sexual and gender minorities wasn't just theoretical; it was something Christians explicitly practiced. We see this clearly in Acts 8: "Now an angel of the Lord said to Philip, 'Go south to the road—the desert road—that goes down from Jerusalem to Gaza.' So he started out, and on his way he met an Ethiopian eunuch, an important official in charge of all the treasury of the Kandake (which means 'queen of the Ethiopians'). This man had gone to Jerusalem to worship, and on his way home was sitting in his chariot reading the Book of Isaiah the prophet" (8:26–28).

Philip, who is one of the main leaders in the first-century church, is told by an angel of the Lord to go and meet a person we come to know as the Ethiopian eunuch. As we have discussed, there were many reasons someone became known as a eunuch, but what is most important to understand is that the Ethiopian eunuch, being what we would now consider a sexual and gender minority, would not have been allowed to enter any assembly where God was worshiped. Jewish law strictly forbade it.[16]

So the Ethiopian eunuch had journeyed about fifteen hundred miles from his home to worship God in community, only to be turned away. Only to be told no one wanted him there. Only to

16. "No one whose testicles are crushed or whose male organ is cut off shall enter the assembly of the Lord" (Deut. 23:1 ESV).

be called unclean and defiled and an abomination. Put yourself in his shoes. Think about how he must have felt. He travels for weeks in pursuit of the God he's been reading about, and when he arrives, the people representing this God completely shun him. For many of you in the LGBTQ+ community, you don't have to imagine; you've experienced such shunning firsthand.

But even after all of that, the eunuch is still reading Scripture on his way home, still pursuing God even though he's been told, "You can never be included." God obviously knows what has happened to the Ethiopian eunuch, and that's why he sends Philip to meet him. "The Spirit of God told Philip, 'Go to that chariot and stay near it.' Then Philip ran up to the chariot and heard the man reading Isaiah the prophet. 'Do you understand what you are reading?' Philip asked. And he said, 'How can I, unless someone explains it to me?'" (Acts 8:29–31). This question from the Ethiopian eunuch is one of the most powerful sentences in all of Scripture and a searing indictment against how the church has so often mistreated LGBTQ+ people.

"How can I possibly understand it?" he asks. In essence he's saying, "I traveled fifteen hundred miles, tried to worship with you all, and asked everyone I met, but no one would explain it to me."

I've lost count of the number of LGBTQ+ folks who have asked me if they're allowed to be a part of God's family even though they are queer. And after I say, "Yes, of course you are!" I always ask, "Have you ever asked any other Christians or pastors that question?"

And do you know how most people respond? They tell me they've tried to ask, but instead of receiving an answer, they are dismissed or condemned.

"How can I understand it? No one will explain it to me."

Like so many sexual and gender minorities I know, the Ethiopian eunuch is undeterred. Even after experiencing bigotry and exclusion, he still wants to be a part of God's family. So God sends Philip to welcome him in with open arms. At the eunuch's request, Philip climbs into the chariot and starts talking with him about what he's reading: "Philip began with that very passage of Scripture and told him the good news about Jesus. As they traveled along the road, they came to some water and the eunuch said, 'Look, here is water. What can stand in the way of my being baptized?'" (Acts 8:35–36).

When Philip hears this question, I'm sure the first thing that goes through his mind is something like "A lot could stand in the way of you being baptized." Basically, every single thing about the Ethiopian eunuch could have been used to keep him from being baptized: his ethnicity, his occupation, his citizenship, and most of all, his being a eunuch.

I cannot overstate what an important moment this is in the history of the church. Because the real question being asked here is this: "Who can be included in God's family?" After all, that's what baptism represents: full inclusion in both God's family and a church family. It's one thing to read Scripture with someone, but it's another thing to wholeheartedly welcome them in through baptism. Philip could have easily pointed out any of those excluding factors and said, "I'm sorry, I can't baptize you." But he doesn't. "Philip said, 'If you believe with all your heart, you may.' The eunuch answered, 'I believe that Jesus Christ is the Son of God.' And he gave orders to stop the chariot. Then both Philip and the eunuch went down into the water and Philip baptized him" (Acts 8:37–38).

My favorite part of this incredible story is that the text says three different times that Philip is directed by God. Why? Because God wants to make sure that everyone who reads this understands that the full inclusion of all people in the family of God, whether they fit the sexual and gender norms of the time or not, is God's idea.

I also like to think that God uses the Scriptures to encourage the Ethiopian eunuch on his journey. Remember, he's reading the book of Isaiah as he bumps along the road in his chariot. Even after he is excluded, I believe God uses those verses from Isaiah 56 to reassure him of his unwavering love for him: "For this is what the LORD says: 'To the eunuchs who keep my Sabbaths, who choose what pleases me and hold fast to my covenant—to them I will give within my temple and its walls a memorial and a name better than sons and daughters; I will give them an everlasting name that will endure forever'" (Isa. 56:4–5).

But What About the Clobber Verses?

The main objection to full inclusion of sexual and gender minorities in the church is made using a handful of verses (three in the Old Testament and three in the New Testament) that seem to prohibit homosexual behavior. These passages are often called "clobber verses," given the way they have been used like weapons against LGBTQ+ folks.

There are two major viewpoints when it comes to interpreting these six verses. The first is non-affirming theology, which holds that Scripture forbids homosexual behavior. Most non-affirming theologians don't focus on the three Old Testament passages in their arguments because one is about Sodom and Gomorrah—a really bizarre story about a group of men attempting to force themselves on angels, which Scripture explicitly says is not about homosexuality[17]—and the other two are part of the Levitical law, by which Christians don't abide.[18] It's also worth

17. "Now this was the sin of your sister Sodom: She and her daughters were arrogant, overfed and unconcerned; they did not help the poor and needy. They were haughty and did detestable things before me. Therefore I did away with them as you have seen" (Ezek. 16:49–50).

18. The Levitical law also includes commands like don't eat pork, don't cut your sideburns, and don't mix your fabrics.

mentioning that Philo, a first-century contemporary of Paul, believed that the Leviticus prohibitions were condemnations of the sexual exploitation of children by adult males.[19]

But non-affirming people interpret the three New Testament verses at face value. The most popular of these verses is in one of Paul's letters to the church in Corinth. Paul says, "Don't you realize that those who do wrong will not inherit the Kingdom of God? Don't fool yourselves. Those who indulge in sexual sin, or who worship idols, or commit adultery, or are male prostitutes, or practice homosexuality, or are thieves, or greedy people, or drunkards, or are abusive, or cheat people—none of these will inherit the Kingdom of God" (1 Cor. 6:9–10 NLT). Non-affirming theologians look at a passage like this and say, "This is a list of bad things we aren't supposed to do. Homosexuality is on this list, so homosexuality must be a bad thing we aren't supposed to do."

To be fair, this is a reasonable reading at face value, and it's the way this passage has often been interpreted. It's also worth pointing out that some LGBTQ+ people hold to this theology and choose to practice celibacy because they believe homosexual behavior is sinful based on long-standing interpretations of these verses.

As you can probably guess, the opposite of non-affirming theology is affirming theology, which claims that Scripture does not teach that LGBTQ+ people or relationships are inherently sinful. The foundational belief of affirming theology is that the "homosexuality" forbidden in Scripture is not the same thing as the loving and equitable same-sex relationships we see today.

Instead, the homosexuality to which Paul refers is about power and abuse and unrestrained lust. In the patriarchal

19. Philo, *Special Laws* 3, trans. F. H. Colson (Harvard University Press, 1939), 39–40.

culture of the first century, men had all the power. They could have sex with their wives, male and female prostitutes, or even male and female slaves without ramifications. There were also pagan temples, like the Temple of Aphrodite in the city of Corinth, where Paul sent this letter, that were famous for encouraging sex as a form of worship. These temples often kept both adults and children as sex slaves.

An affirming interpretation of this passage claims that those exploitative practices are what Scripture is condemning and that we should still condemn those things today. Affirming theology argues that loving and equitable same-sex relationships as we understand and see them in modern times did not exist in the biblical world, and that is historically accurate. Many non-affirming scholars concede that point, but they nonetheless believe that Scripture still forbids homosexual activity.

Numerous biblical scholars note that the word "homosexuality" did not appear in any English Bible translation until 1946, when the committee working on the Revised Standard Version (RSV) translated two Greek words as the English word "homosexuality" in 1 Corinthians 6:9–10. The words had previously been translated as "abusers of themselves with mankind" (KJV; cf. ASV), "effeminate" (NASB 1995), or "boy molester" (cf. Luther Bible), lending further credence to the belief that Paul is condemning pederasty[20] and other exploitative sexual practices.

Conflating these practices with the more general "homosexuality" in the RSV translation was a mistake. Not long after the RSV was published, a twenty-one-year-old seminary student named David S. Fearon sent a letter to the committee disputing their translation. Luther Weigle, the head of the committee, responded with a letter acknowledging their mistake and

20. A sexual "relationship" between an adult male and a male child practiced frequently in ancient Greco-Roman culture.

committing to correct the error, but "homosexuality" wasn't officially changed to the more accurate "sexual perversions" until the next revision was published in 1971. After twenty-five years, the damage was done. "Homosexuality" had been picked up by other translations and applied to other New Testament verses too.[21]

Queer exclusion in the church was all I knew for much of my young life. Growing up Southern Baptist meant I spent my adolescence in very anti-LGBTQ+ spaces. To be honest, I'm not exactly sure when I woke up to God's radical inclusion. It wasn't like a switch that flipped; it was more like a dam that slowly developed cracks until the whole thing finally gave way.

The cracks started forming in college when I met LGBTQ+ folks who deeply loved and pursued God. The cracks became bigger when I met queer Christians who had suffered the horrors of conversion therapy but still faithfully followed Jesus. They got even bigger when I met people who had been kicked out of churches because of their sexual orientation or gender identity and yet still wanted to be part of a church family.[22] And then, when I began to dig deeply into Scripture, the dam burst. I began to apply the same interpretive lenses to the six passages about homosexuality that I did to everything else in Scripture, and when I did, it became apparent that the "homosexuality" being forbidden in the Bible bears no resemblance to the loving, equitable, Spirit-filled same-sex relationships of my queer siblings in Christ.[23]

21. The excellent documentary *1946* tells the whole story. You can learn more and watch the film at https://www.1946themovie.com.

22. Acts 10 and 15 are great examples of early Christians changing their minds about who is included in God's family in a similar way. Acts 15:8 says, "God, who knows the heart, showed that he accepted them by giving the Holy Spirit to them, just as he did to us."

23. If you want to dive deeper into affirming theology, here is a list of resources I recommend: Brownson, *Bible, Gender, and Sexuality*; DeFranza, *Sex Difference in Christian Theology*; David P. Gushee, *Changing Our Mind*, 3rd ed. (Read the Spirit, 2017); Austen Hartke, *Transforming: The Bible and the Lives of Transgender Christians* (Westminster

I do not believe that same-sex relationships are inherently sinful. They can be, but only in the same way a heterosexual relationship can be—when there isn't respect, equality, and Christ-centered love in the middle of it.[24] Regardless of one's gender or sexual orientation, the apostle Paul calls Christian spouses to live in mutual submission to each other (Eph. 5:21). I'm not advocating for the abolition of covenantal, Christian marriages. I am advocating for the church to include our LGBTQ+ siblings in those relationships. I really like the way biblical ethicist David Gushee puts it:

> If what we are talking about is blessing an anything-goes ethic in a morally libertine culture, I stand utterly opposed, as I have throughout my career. But if what we are talking about is carving out space for serious committed Christians who happen to be gay or lesbian, to participate in society as equals, in church as kin, and in the blessings and demands of covenant on the same terms as everyone else, I now think that has nothing to do with cultural, ecclesial and moral decline, and everything to do with treating people the way Christ did.[25]

I want to be absolutely clear: I believe in affirming theology because of Jesus and Scripture, not in spite of them. I believe in

---

John Knox, 2023); Karen Keen, *Scripture, Ethics, and the Possibility of Same-Sex Relationships* (Eerdmans, 2018); Mihee Kim-Kort, *Outside the Lines: How Embracing Queerness Will Transform Your Faith* (Fortress, 2018); Colby Martin, *UnClobber: Rethinking Our Misuse of the Bible on Homosexuality* (Westminster John Knox, 2022); Matthew Vines, *God and the Gay Christian: The Biblical Case in Support of Same-Sex Relationships* (Convergent, 2015). For an excellent and concise overview of how affirming theology engages with common non-affirming arguments and Scripture, see "Brief Biblical Case for LGBTQ Inclusion," Reformation Project, accessed January 7, 2025, https://reformationproject.org/biblical-case.

24. An important side note: I don't believe heterosexual or homosexual marriage is a necessary part of life. Singleness is good and beautiful. Single people are not incomplete. They do not reflect any less of God's image or fulfill any less of God's mission without a spouse or partner.

25. Gushee, *Changing Our Mind*, 115.

it because of the toxic fruit I've seen come from marginalizing and excluding the queer community. And I believe in it because of the good fruit I've seen come from fully affirming LGBTQ+ folks as they follow Jesus and lead in the church.

This is the fruitfulness lens at work. I've seen love, joy, peace, forbearance, kindness, goodness, faithfulness, gentleness, and self-control come from interpreting Scripture in an affirming way so many times, but one of my favorite stories is about my friend Kayla.

"What the Hell Else Was I Gonna Do?"

I met Kayla about seven years ago. She'd moved to Austin to pursue her doctorate in physical therapy and was part of a group from her school who started coming to Restore. Not long after we met, she asked if we could get together for coffee. I soon found myself sitting across the table from her at a café on a hot, early fall day in Austin. As we sipped our lattes, she told me something she'd told only a couple of other people—she was gay.

Growing up in church, Kayla had heard all the clobber verses. At that point in her life, she was pretty sure her sexual orientation was a sin, but she'd prayed for God to change her, and he hadn't. So what now?

I asked her how I could best support her, and she asked me if we could pray together. "Of course," I said. "What do you want to pray for, Kayla?"

She said she wanted us to pray that God's will would happen in her life, no matter what it was. Whether it was an orientation change or a life of celibacy or something else entirely, she said she just wanted God's best for her life. So that's what we did. We prayed for God's best.

We prayed this together periodically for a few uneventful months, and I could tell that God's seeming lack of direction in her life was really weighing on her. So one day I asked if she'd ever considered that God's best might not be an orientation change or an uncoupled life—that God might have an incredible woman out there for her to fall in love with and marry?

She teared up and said something like "That sounds too good to be true." A few weeks later, as the band played our closing song one Sunday morning, she came up to me and asked if we could pray again. "I want to pray for God to introduce me to that woman we talked about, but only if it's his will," she said. So that's what we prayed from then on—that God would bring her a woman who loves her, who loves Jesus, and with whom she could build a life.

And God did exactly that. When Kayla met Hannah, she knew pretty quickly that this was the woman we'd been praying for. After they got engaged, Kayla texted me and said, "I am so thankful for being introduced to Restore and that day we prayed together. It's a moment I reflect on frequently when looking at where I am today. Thank you so much."

A couple of years ago, I had the incredible honor of officiating their wedding. It was a wonderful day, but my favorite part was seeing their family and friends there to support them. I had a chance to chat with Kayla's dad for a few minutes during the reception. He grew up in the Bible Belt and had previously been taught the same anti-LGBTQ+ theology as Kayla, so I asked him what his journey had been like.

He said, "Did you know she came out to me in my pickup truck at the deer lease?" I didn't, so I asked him how it had gone. He described the scene for me. She was back home visiting, and they were driving down a back road headed toward their deer blind. During a quiet moment, Kayla told him she was gay and that she'd met someone.

"Wow. What did you say?" I asked with bated breath.

He kind of looked up at the sky to recall the moment, then he turned to me and said, "I told her I was happy for her, that

I've always loved her and I always will, no matter what." Then he turned to me and shrugged. "I'm her dad and I love her so much. What the hell else was I gonna do?"

Toxic Fruit Transformed

I put a lot of really sobering statistics into the first part of this chapter, but I want to share one more with you that I find to be so encouraging. When it comes to those who have left the church as adults, only 9 percent say they are open to returning. But do you know what the percentage of LGBTQ+ folks who say they are open to coming back to church is? Seventy-six percent![26]

More than three-quarters of queer folks who have left the church are open to coming back if they can find a safe, inclusive, healthy, Jesus-centered community to be a part of. A place where they can fully participate. A place where they can be fully known, share their gifts, and lead. This is exactly what we've seen at Restore. According to our last survey, 30 percent of our church members belong to the LGBTQ+ community.

This is not tokenization. This isn't posting a rainbow flag on our church Facebook page every June and pretending like that makes us a safe space. This is co-laboring. This is queer folks leading and influencing and flourishing in their exercise of diverse spiritual gifts. And all of this isn't just a blessing for LGBTQ+ people; it is an immense blessing for our church. Bible interpretations that bear bad fruit have not only harmed queer folks; they have also messed up the church. When we exclude the people God tells us to include, we miss out on the gifts and talents they bring; we miss out on the unique ways in which they bear God's image; and we miss out on the fruit of the Spirit they express. What Christians have too often done to the LGBTQ+

26. Marin, *Us Versus Us*, 65.

community is like the body of Christ cutting off an arm or a leg. We are incomplete without them.

For two thousand years, sexual and gender minorities have been doing their best to follow Jesus, and many Christians have been too blinded by bad Bible interpretations to notice. For too long, churches have tried to take Jesus from LGBTQ+ people. I am committed to doing everything I can to make that stop. Not in spite of Jesus and the Bible but because of them.

If we are going to take seriously Jesus's call to be people who produce good fruit, then we must lead with love, inclusion, and affirmation. We must build tables where everyone has a seat, and we must create spaces of mutual flourishing where queer people and straight people participate and lead alongside each other. As Kayla's dad said so perfectly, "What the hell else are we gonna do?"

Putting on the fruitfulness lens helps us avoid the mistakes that have led Christians to produce poisonous fruit in the past. It also helps us transform that toxic fruit into what Jesus said his followers should be known for: love, joy, peace, forbearance, kindness, goodness, faithfulness, gentleness, and self-control.

conclusion

A Restored Reading

> The only clear line I draw these days is this: when my religion tries to come between me and my neighbor, I will choose my neighbor. . . . Jesus never commanded me to love my religion.
>
> —Barbara Brown Taylor, *Holy Envy*

I was outside one of my favorite Indian food spots in Austin on May 24, 2022, when I got word of the shooting at Robb Elementary School in Uvalde, Texas. I'd just finished lunch with a church member when I walked out to my car, opened my phone, and saw text messages from friends and family alerting me to the news.

Tragedies like this hit everyone hard, but I fell apart. Not only did I have elementary-school-aged children, but my grandmother Jo Claire was born and raised in Uvalde. I'd been there many times, spending hours running around her childhood home just a few short blocks from the school. I talked to our pastoral team at Restore later that day, and we made plans to include a time of lament and prayer in our Sunday gathering that week. I was supposed to preach the sermon and then make my way over to our prayer station to pray with anyone who wanted to.

When Sunday came, I could barely get through the sermon. If you've ever listened to me preach, you know I'll occasionally get choked up, but this was something different. I stumbled and sobbed my way through the final few minutes before walking over to the prayer station. The very last thing I wanted to do in that moment was pray for someone else. I had nothing left. I stood at the station with my head bowed, praying for a good thirty seconds that no one would come over, but when I looked up, a dozen people were in line to pray.

My heart sank, but I steeled myself as best I could and waved the first person forward. Her name is Sharon, and she's been a member of our church for years. Sharon walked up, wrapped me in a big hug, and said, "I didn't come so you could pray for me. I came to pray for you." I immediately started crying, and she prayed over me. And she wasn't the only one—ten of the twelve people in line said something similar and prayed for me too.

Moments like that help me remember the vital necessity that is a loving community. We can be incredible Bible scholars, have all the right interpretive lenses, and memorize Scripture until the cows come home, but if we don't have people who love us and are loved by us, none of it matters. Paul famously says something similar about love: "If I speak in the tongues of men or of angels, but do not have love, I am only a resounding gong or a clanging cymbal. If I have the gift of prophecy and can fathom all mysteries and all knowledge, and if I have a faith that can move mountains, but do not have love, I am nothing. If I give all I possess to the poor and give over my body to hardship that I may boast, but do not have love, I gain nothing. . . . Now these three remain: faith, hope and love. But the greatest of these is love" (1 Cor. 13:1–3, 13).

We Need Each Other

The Bible has always been the church's book. It belongs to the people and is best interpreted within a healthy and diverse community. That's how I know that the lenses I've been talking about promote healing rather than inflicting harm. Not because a scholar said so or because I cracked some code, but because I've seen them bring healing, wholeness, and flourishing to our community at Restore for a decade.

Reading the Bible alongside a healthy and diverse community helps us see the Scriptures through other people's eyes. This community is not only other Christians we know but also Christians throughout time who have written about the Bible and theology. We can get into trouble pretty easily when we make all our interpretive decisions in isolation or only with people who look, think, and believe exactly like we do.

We are better when we are all together. We make better decisions, we hurt fewer people inadvertently, and we more fully represent the image of God when we belong to a healthy and diverse community. Consider Matthew 26:7–11, a passage often used by those who advocate against helping people in poverty: "A woman came to [Jesus] with an alabaster jar of very expensive perfume, which she poured on his head as he was reclining at the table. When the disciples saw this, they were indignant. 'Why this waste?' they asked. 'This perfume could have been sold at a high price and the money given to the poor.' Aware of this, Jesus said to them, 'Why are you bothering this woman? She has done a beautiful thing to me. The poor you will always have with you, but you will not always have me.'"

The statement "the poor you will always have with you" has been used to justify neglecting the poor for hundreds of years. But if this passage were interpreted alongside people in poverty, they would immediately point out that it can't mean that. Jesus can't be talking about ignoring the poor, because he came to bring freedom and flourishing to all people, especially those on the margins. So what is a better interpretation?

Well, Jesus is actually quoting the Hebrew Scriptures. Here is the full verse: "There will always be poor people in the land. Therefore I command you to be openhanded toward your fellow Israelites who are poor and needy in your land" (Deut. 15:11).

Jesus is reminding his followers of their responsibility to give freely to the poor, not providing them an excuse to ignore them. Jesus isn't advocating against helping people in poverty. Far from it. Instead, a better interpretation is that Jesus is commending this woman for her generosity toward him while also reminding everyone in the room of their responsibility to share freely with the poor among them.

This new and better interpretation demonstrates the power of employing all four healthy lenses we've been talking about:

- The Jesus lens reminds us that in Jesus's very first sermon, the one in which he lays out his mission, he says, "The Spirit of the Lord is on me, because he has anointed me to proclaim good news to the poor" (Luke 4:18). If Jesus came to proclaim good news to the poor, then he wouldn't advocate neglecting them.
- The context lens helps us look at the context of the quote Jesus is referencing here to better understand the culture and background.
- The flourishing lens emphasizes that an interpretation that further marginalizes anyone, including the poor, is wrong.

- The fruitfulness lens prompts us to evaluate whether an interpretation produces love, joy, peace, forbearance, kindness, goodness, faithfulness, gentleness, and self-control. Indifference to folks in need doesn't produce any good fruit.

But all these lenses will ultimately fall short without the encouragement and perspective of a healthy and diverse community. I love how Kaitlyn Schiess says it: "We actually do need more than a Bible and our own minds. We need each other."[1]

When the Bible Becomes a Tool of Healing

I have seen so much goodness come as harmful lenses have fallen from the eyes of people in our church and been replaced by better ways to read the Bible. Many of these folks' stories are in the previous chapters, but I could easily fill a dozen more books.

When I think of harmful lenses falling off, I think of my friend Javier. He grew up in a church with Philippians 4:13—"I can do all things through him who gives me strength"—painted on a wall in the sanctuary. He never knew his dad, but his mom took him and his little sisters to church every time the doors were open. She diligently tithed, even though her income was meager, and she volunteered in the nursery every Sunday morning.

"She's the most faithful person I have ever known," Javier once told me. But when Javier was sixteen, his mom got sick. The doctor diagnosed her with stage 4 cervical cancer and gave her six months to live.

The first place they went after the doctor's office was their church. Javier's mom wanted the pastor to pray over her. She sat in a church pew right underneath that painting of Philippians

1. Kaitlyn Schiess, *The Ballot and the Bible: How Scripture Has Been Used and Abused in American Politics and Where We Go from Here* (Brazos, 2023), 34.

4:13 as the pastor laid hands on her and prayed. Javier still remembers the pastor's prayer: "Dear God, your Word says that we can do all things through Christ who strengthens us, so we know that through the power of Christ, this woman is going to beat cancer and experience miraculous healing."

Four months later, Javier's mom passed away.

Javier's faith was destroyed. He walked away from church and from God. Justo González calls the kind of biblical interpretation undergirding the pastor's prayer a "dangerous illusion,"[2] because when an illusion like this breaks, it doesn't just hurt one person. It shatters like a sheet of glass—shards go everywhere and people get cut by the broken pieces.

Two decades later, Javier found himself sitting at one of Restore's Sunday gatherings. Dragged there by his girlfriend, Maria (Javier told me later that Maria was the only reason he stepped foot back in a church), he heard a sermon about reading the Bible in context. Javier walked up to me afterward and asked if there was context for Philippians 4:13. I had no idea why he was asking me this, but I responded, "Yes, there's context around every verse in the Bible." Javier asked if we could talk more about it, so I pulled out my phone to schedule a meeting, but when I looked up at him, his eyes were filled with tears. I asked if he wanted to talk right then, and he nodded. So Javier, Maria, and I went to the lobby and sat down.

Maria was holding her Bible, so I asked if she would open it to Philippians 4. She did so and then handed it to me. I quickly explained that Philippians is a letter written by a persecutor of Christians turned pastor, named Paul. We know from the first chapter of this letter that Paul is writing from prison. He writes this letter to the church in Philippi mostly as a kind of thank-you

2. Justo L. González, *Santa Biblia: The Bible Through Hispanic Eyes* (Abingdon, 1996), 13.

note for their support of him during difficult times, but he also spends part of the letter offering encouragement of his own.

Chapter 4 is the last section of this letter. In it, Paul reminds his audience to "rejoice always" and bring all their worries to God in prayer. He promises that God's peace is always available to them, no matter what they face. And then we come to the section that houses the infamous Philippians 4:13. Paul thanks them again for the support they've sent and then writes, "I have learned to be content whatever the circumstances. I know what it is to be in need, and I know what it is to have plenty. I have learned the secret of being content in any and every situation, whether well fed or hungry, whether living in plenty or in want. I can do all this through him who gives me strength" (4:11–13).

I laid Maria's Bible down on the table between us and waited. Javier wasn't looking at me or Maria. His eyes were fixed, unblinking, on the open Bible. It felt like a full minute passed in silence before Javier muttered in disbelief, "How have I never heard that?"

Paul isn't casting God as some magical genie who grants our every wish. He's not saying that God will get us a job promotion or heal our cancer if we pray hard enough. He's not promising a life of blessings if we follow all God's rules. Paul is saying that his faith in Jesus empowers him to endure any circumstance, no matter how difficult. Paul can be content in any situation, even prison, through the encouragement of Christ and his fellow Christians. Jesus gives him strength when he has none left of his own.

The truth of that message is what resonated with Javier all those years later. When he found himself imprisoned by grief after the death of his mom and angry at the God he thought refused to save her, this message of hope amid pain helped heal his broken heart.

Bad Bible interpretation hurts people, but the answer to bad Bible interpretation isn't throwing away the Scriptures. The answer to bad Bible interpretation is good Bible interpretation. When harmful lenses are replaced by healthy ones, we can deconstruct the ways we've been harmed by Scripture and used it to harm others. Stories like Javier's and so many others throughout this book are why I believe strongly in the power of Jesus working through Scripture to promote wholeness and flourishing in our lives.

The Bible has been used to inflict harm on many of us. This has often left us feeling powerless when it comes to reading Scripture; we don't even want to open the Bible because we are so afraid or anxious or triggered. But we are not without agency when it comes to reading and understanding the Bible. We can transform it into a tool of healing. We just need to know what we're looking for. Rachel Held Evans once wrote:

> The truth is, you can bend Scripture to say just about anything you want it to say. You can bend it until it breaks. For those who count the Bible as sacred, interpretation is not a matter of whether to pick and choose, but how to pick and choose. We're all selective. We all wrestle with how to interpret and apply the Bible to our lives. We all go to the text looking for something, and we all have a tendency to find it. So the question we have to ask ourselves is this: are we reading with the prejudice of love, with Christ as our model, or are we reading with the prejudices of judgment and power, self-interest and greed? Are we seeking to enslave or liberate, burden or set free?
>
> If you are looking for Bible verses with which to support slavery, you will find them. If you are looking for verses with which to abolish slavery, you will find them. If you are looking for verses with which to oppress women, you will find them. If you are looking for verses with which to honor and celebrate women, you will find them. If you are looking for reasons to wage war,

> there are plenty. If you are looking for reasons to promote peace, there are plenty more. If you are looking for an outdated and irrelevant ancient text, that's exactly what you will see. If you are looking for truth, that's exactly what you will find.
>
> If you want to do violence in this world, you will always find the weapons. If you want to heal, you will always find the balm. With Scripture, we've been entrusted with some of the most powerful stories ever told. How we harness that power, whether for good or evil, oppression or liberation, changes everything.[3]

I hope this book is a balm. I pray the stories and concepts found in these pages will help you read the Bible in ways that bring healing and wholeness for yourself and your neighbor. Transformation can happen. I've seen it and experienced it firsthand too many times for me to doubt it now. I know it might feel like your love of Scripture is dead or your faith is lifeless, but Jesus is in the business of resurrection.

You can be transformed. The people you love can be transformed. Your parent who has bought into the lie of religious hierarchy and spends their time supporting a version of Christianity consumed with power and domination can embrace the way of Jesus. Your child who has been wounded by moralistic doctrine can heal from the damage of legalism. Your partner who has walked away from faith because they find literalistic interpretations of the creation story preposterous can find a faith that works with science instead of against it. Your friend who has fallen into conspiracy theories based on Left Behind theology can be set free.

There are better ways to read the Bible than what many of us have been taught—ways that lead to liberation and fullness of life for absolutely everyone.

3. Rachel Held Evans, *Inspired: Slaying Giants, Walking on Water, and Loving the Bible Again* (Thomas Nelson, 2018), 57–58.

acknowledgments

Acknowledgments always feel like an Oscars acceptance speech, but without the music to cut you off when you've gone on too long. In that spirit, I'll do my best to keep this brief.

First and foremost, I want to thank my partner, Amy. I shared some of our story in chapter 8, so I won't rehash it here except to say that nothing in my life would be possible without her. Amy, you are my guiding light, my intellectual superior, and my best friend. I've loved you since I was eleven years old, and I will never stop.

I also want to thank my two sons. They were not the reason we moved back to Austin to plant Restore, but they are a huge reason I keep getting out of bed every day to do this work. They have no category for a faith community that doesn't pursue justice, equality, and flourishing for all people. They've never been a part of a church that has restrictions based on someone's age, race, gender, or sexual orientation. Watching you both grow into kind, caring, and brilliant humans is a joy. I am so lucky to be your dad.

Thank you to my agent and friend, Jonathan Merritt, who believed in this project from the beginning and led me through every part of the process with tremendous skill and patience. Thank you to my editor, Katelyn Beaty, for her diligence and expertise. You are the main reason we chose Brazos Press, and it was absolutely the right call. Thank you to Brian Vos, Erin Smith, Eric Salo, and the rest of the Brazos Press team. You all have made this book better, and I am deeply grateful.

I want to thank my extended family as well. To my parents, Reagan and Debbie: Thank you for teaching me to love Jesus, the Bible, and the church. I am forever grateful for the faith foundation you gave me. To my in-laws, Fla and Nadine: Thank you for your relentless support over the past twenty years. To the Jacksons, Ruples, and Strawns: Thank you for your encouragement and for always being willing to play overly competitive games during family holidays.

Thank you to the mentors and friends who have helped me along the way in ministry and specifically with this writing process: David Gushee, Karen Keen, Sally Gary, Trey Ferguson, Pete Briscoe, Lisa Sharon Harper, and others—many of whom are listed at the end of chapter 1. Thank you to Dan Lowery and Zack McCoy. When the writer of Proverbs 18:24 says, "There is a friend who sticks closer than a brother," he is talking about you two. We have been through so much together over the last decade, and I wouldn't trade it for anything. Thank you to Matt and Emily Gonzalez. You stepped out in faith and moved to Austin to help start Restore from scratch. I will never get over that. All these years later, we are still in this together, and I wouldn't want it any other way.

Finally, thank you to the people of Restore. You have been an integral part of this journey, and your impact on this book and my life cannot be overstated. Your stories inspire me daily, and I'm deeply grateful for the opportunity to share many of them with the world through this book. Being a pastor at Restore is one of the greatest gifts in my life. The way you've embraced me, my family, and this work has been a constant reminder of the transformative power of healthy, diverse, Jesus-centered community. Thank you for being a living example of how faith communities can foster healing and wholeness. I want to especially thank the pastors I get to lead alongside: Matt Gonzalez, Lindsay Contreras, Mark Jordan, Sonja DiNanno, and Kelsie Rogers. Each of you embodies the way of Jesus in such unique and diverse ways. I'm a better pastor and person because of y'all.

To all those who have grappled with their faith and sought better ways to read the Bible, this book is for you. May it contribute to a world where Scripture is used as God intended—to promote healing, wholeness, and flourishing for all.

zach w. lambert

is the lead pastor and founder of Restore Austin, a church in Austin, Texas. Under his leadership, Restore has grown from a launch team of five people in 2015 to more than one thousand members today. He has a master of theology from Dallas Theological Seminary and is pursuing his doctorate at Duke Divinity School. Zach is the cofounder of the Post-Evangelical Collective, where he serves as a board member. He also serves on the boards of the Austin Church Planting Network and the Multi-Faith Neighbors Network. Zach lives in Austin with his wife, Amy, and their two sons.

Connect with Zach

zachwlambert

@zachwlambert

@zachwlambert

@ZachWLambert